HOW TO MAKE MOVIES
A Practical Guide to Group Film-Making

HOW TO MAKE MOVIES
A Practical Guide to Group Film-Making

Robert Ferguson

A Studio Book

THE VIKING PRESS New York

Acknowledgments

QUOTATIONS

P 23 and p 53: 'The Writer and the Film' by
Dudley Nichols from *Film – A Montage of Theories*,
Dutton Paperback, E. P. Dutton, New York, 1966
(appeared originally in *Great Film Plays*, John
Gassener and Dudley Nichols [ed.] Crown Pub-
lishers, New York; p 27: from an article by Howard
Hawkes published in *Movie Magazine*; p 29: the
preface from *Two for the Road* by Frederic Raphael,
Jonathan Cape, London, 1967 and Holt, Rinehart
and Winston, New York; p 37: from an article by
Alfred Hitchcock from *Film – A Montage of
Theories*, Dutton Paperback, E. P. Dutton, New
York, 1968 (appeared originally in *Great Film
Plays*, John Gassener and Dudley Nichols [ed.]
Crown Publishers, New York; p 51: 'Direction' by
Alfred Hitchcock from *Footnotes to the Film*, Charles
Davy [ed.] Peter Davies, London; p 70: from an
article by Walter Lassally published in *Sight and
Sound*, 1965; p 77: Harold Pinter from an inter-
view with John Russell Taylor published in *Sight
and Sound*, 1966.

ILLUSTRATIONS

For the stills on pages 44, 45, 47, 50, 53, 68 thanks
are due to the following distributors: George de
Beauregard, Paris; Columbia Pictures and to the
British Film Institute.

Published in Great Britain 1969 by Studio Vista Publishers
Blue Star House, Highgate Hill, London N19
and in the USA 1969 by The Viking Press, Inc.
625 Madison Avenue, New York, NY 10022
Library of Congress catalog card number: 69–17872
Set in 12 pt Modern No. 7
Printed in Great Britain by Fletcher and Son Ltd., Norwich

UK ISBN 0 289 79574 5 (hardbound)
    ISBN 0 289 70305 0 (paperbound)

USA SBN 670–38440–2 (hardbound)
    SBN 670–02025–7 (paperbound)

Contents

Introduction

This book, based on practical experience gained through film work in schools, colleges, youth clubs, and working at a semi-professional level, is written as an introductory guide for any group of people who come together with the idea of making serious use of the medium. The general approach is valid irrespective of the gauge of film used, the age range, or the size of the group. What is offered is a way of *beginning*.

Groups are encouraged to explore their own talents and limitations through experiments with carefully chosen film exercises, and then to develop and modify their approach as they gain experience. Whenever possible, more than one method of tackling a problem is suggested and I hope that it will become apparent that group film work may be, but need not necessarily be, modelled on the lines of the commercial cinema. Pseudo-professionalism does tend to occur in some groups and should be avoided. I have attempted to point out where it might creep in if not checked.

During the years since the war many educational and social organizations have become involved in the use of practical film work. Perhaps many of them have concentrated too much on producing travelogues or story films where the plots are not sufficiently well-developed or the actors not sufficiently experienced – when they would find it both simpler and more exciting to observe and reconstruct a total incident common to everyday life and to their own environment. Young people, in particular, tire quickly of trying to 'make movies' without any clear idea of what they are trying to achieve beyond using a cine-camera in much the same way as they might a still camera, or conversely trying to ape the professional cinema.

For this reason exercises are suggested which may help group members to discover for themselves what they can achieve. From these exercises they can build a vocabulary of film experience. It is then easier to grasp the wide range of possibilities within group film-making.

THE FORMATION OF A FILM GROUP

Some of the most successful groups have been those which grew from an already existent activity, often involving the use of creative drama. It is not so easy to form a group simply by putting up a poster. One may only attract camera fanatics and others who do not help a group get under way. You should, therefore, make a distinction between 'home movies', perhaps made up of holiday material or shots of children on the lawn, and the more ambitious but, in a way, simpler activities of group film-making.

Cameras which may have many technical gimmicks and tape-recorders which record automatically are not necessarily the key to success. Many of the exercises suggested can be done with the cheapest of equipment. The true key to success is to discover your own technical and creative limitations and work within them.

In the past, group film activities have had a clear stratification of jobs and their relative importance. A group member may have been involved in several films but never have touched a camera. The type of groups discussed in the book, however, have been built up so that each member knows what it is like on both sides of the camera and has had experience of writing scripts and directing.

There is no doubt that as a group progresses certain members will show a preference for certain jobs but by this time the choice will not be arbitrary. Members should be willing and able to change jobs according to the particular film being shot.

A wide age range in members can be an asset if one is trying to avoid constant caricature. Most people look their age on the screen. Even the make-up resources of Hollywood have found difficulty in making a young actress look convincingly old.

A film group does not have to be large to be successful. A hard core of eight members is enough. Once the basic film equipment has been purchased, the cost of film stock can be covered by some form of subscription, especially if work is done on 8 mm. or Super 8 film. No special studio space is required, as all films are shot on location. It is no longer necessary to build a living-room and try to make it look real. Film stocks and lighting equipment are available which make it easier to work at the actual location.

THE MOTIVATION OF A FILM GROUP

Motivation for filming is very important. By far the simplest and often the most interesting group films will be about people, so that much of a group's effort should go into the study of people and their portrayal on the screen. There are three main factors which determine how a person looks on film:

The cine-camera records gesture

1 Gesture
2 Movement
3 Facial expression

Groups should devise exercises which consider these factors both separately and together as a cumulative effect. But remember that a balance should be struck between the number of finished films which are produced and the number of genuinely explorative exercises.

The study of feature films is of great value to any group. They should be studied with an attitude of open inquiry rather than awe. Not everything that reaches the commercial screen warrants admiration, but a great deal can be learnt about basic editing simply by concentrating on the way shots are strung together. It is worth sitting through a good film (movie) several times, simply to observe technique.

A purposeful study of professional films is important to any group, and in this connection there are various bodies or educational institutes which can provide information on how to see new and old films. In the U.K. the facilities of The British Film Institute, Education Department, 70 Old Compton Street, London W.1 are worth using. At the same address are the offices of The Society for Education in Film and Television which publishes a bi-monthly magazine, *Screen Education*, dealing with group film work carried out in England and America, at many different levels. There is no single source of information at present in the U.S.A. but one may write or go to the American Film Institute (with offices in Washington D.C., New York City and Los Angeles), the Federation of Film Societies, or the Museum of Modern Art Film Library in New York, or the Academy of Motion Picture Arts and Sciences in Los Angeles.

The cine-camera records movement

9

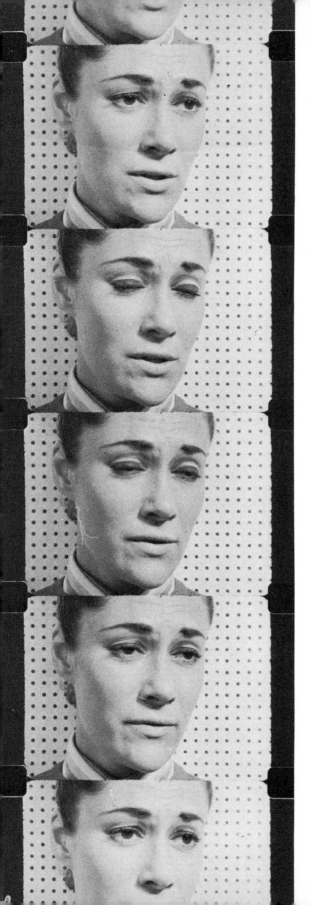

The cine-camera records the subtlest changes in facial expression and gives them life and significance

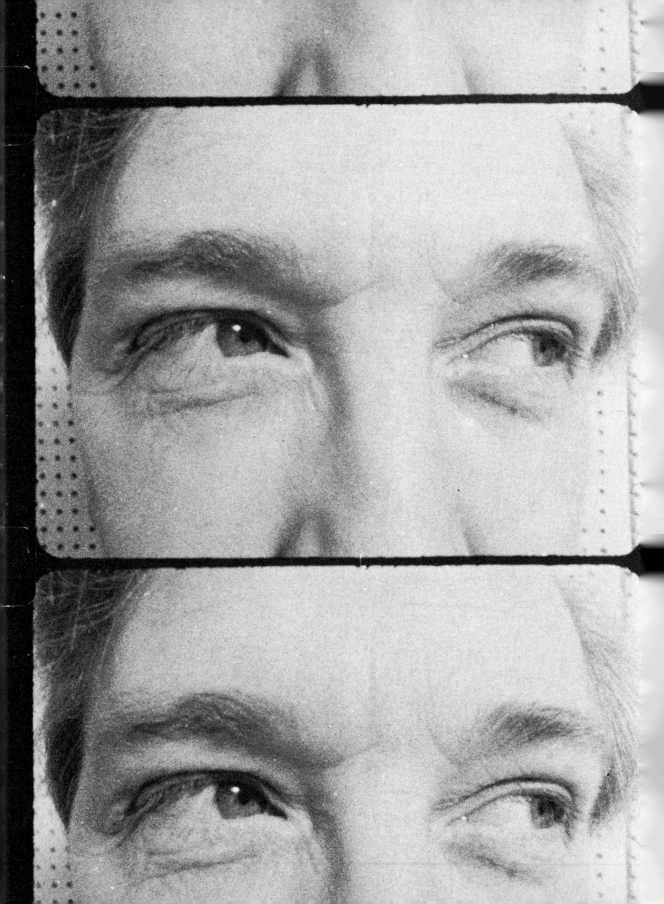

Film-making equipment

The first major problem for any film group is to obtain the necessary basic equipment. It is the aim of this chapter to indicate some of the vast range of cine and sound equipment available to film groups. No detailed technical instruction will be given and stress will be placed on the *types* of equipment which are available.

GAUGES OF FILM

There are three gauges of film which may come within the budget of a film group. These are 16 mm., 8 mm., and Super 8.

16 mm. film

Today 16 mm. film has become almost a professional gauge. You can obtain a complete range of editing and other technical equipment for 16 mm. work. There are also many types of film stock available on this gauge. The film is sold in 100-foot reels, though it can be purchased in 400-foot reels if it is to be used in more expensive cameras which have magazines. It is possible to project film of this gauge on to a full-size cinema screen with very little loss of definition. When projected at 24 f.p.s. 100 feet of 16 mm. film will run for two minutes and forty-seven seconds. If the film is to be silent, it may be shot at 16 or 18 f.p.s., in which case 100 feet will run for over four minutes.

8 mm. film

It is difficult to know how much longer this gauge will remain in existence. 8 mm. cine-cameras are no longer manufactured and must be purchased second-hand. 8 mm. film stock is still on the market in a variety of types in both colour and black and white. This gauge is made by producing 16 mm. film which has double the normal number of perforation holes. The film is run through the camera twice, each time exposing one-half. When the film is processed at the laboratories it is slit down the middle and joined together to make one single strand of 8 mm. film. Film for 8 mm. cameras is available on 25 feet 16 mm. reels which become 50 feet of 8 mm. film after processing. Fifty feet of 8 mm. film runs for roughly four minutes at 16–18 f.p.s.

Super 8 film

This is a comparatively new gauge. It is specially made for Super 8 cameras and is run through only once. One of its main advantages is the size of each picture frame. It has been designed so that it is larger than that of 8 mm film. This makes editing simpler and ensures much better picture quality when projecting. At the moment Super 8 cameras are cassette loaded and there is a limited choice in types of film stock. This situation may well change in the future. A Super 8 film from a cassette lasts a little under four minutes when projected, due to the slightly larger frame size. In order to use this gauge of film all film equipment such as projectors must be Super 8. There are some firms who manufacture equipment which can be adapted to take both 8 mm. and Super 8.

Film stocks

All film stocks, whether black and white or colour are given relative speeds. These speeds are measured on one of several scales. The most common scale is known as A.S.A. preceded by a figure. This figure is always set on the light meter before filming. If the light meter is built into the camera the speed must be set on a control on the camera.

The faster the film the higher the figure. A fast film is one which requires a relatively small amount of light in order to be correctly exposed. Note that the faster a film is, the more grainy a picture is likely to become.

Film speeds are essentially a guide and should not be taken as accurate until a test has been made using the group's own light meter.

Film speeds change for one particular film stock if it is used in daylight and then the lighting is switched to artificial light, i.e., a new meter setting is required.

When using colour film you will have to use different stocks when changing from artificial light to daylight. Alternatively make use of filters which convert one type of stock to another.

Super 8 cameras use only one type of colour film at the moment. The conversion filter is built into the camera and is operated by turning a small lever. Details of the types and purposes of filters may be obtained from any photographic dealers. Such details would not be necessary to a group until it had gained some filming experience.

NEGATIVE/POSITIVE AND REVERSAL FILM

These names refer to the way in which a film is processed. A negative film is one in which the film which runs through the camera is developed to a normal negative. From this negative one or more prints may be taken.

A reversal film is processed in a special way so that it becomes a positive on print. In this case the film which

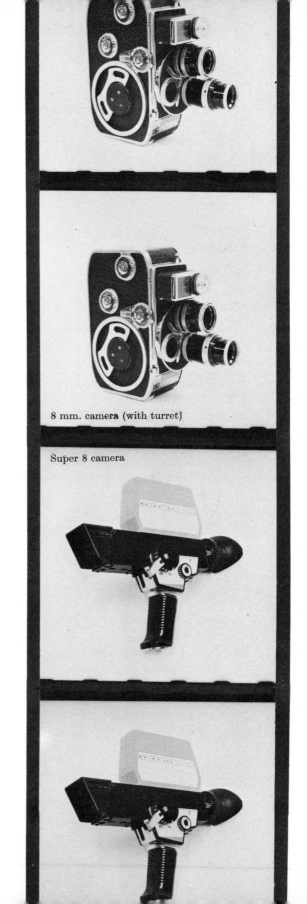

8 mm. camera (with turret)

Super 8 camera

13

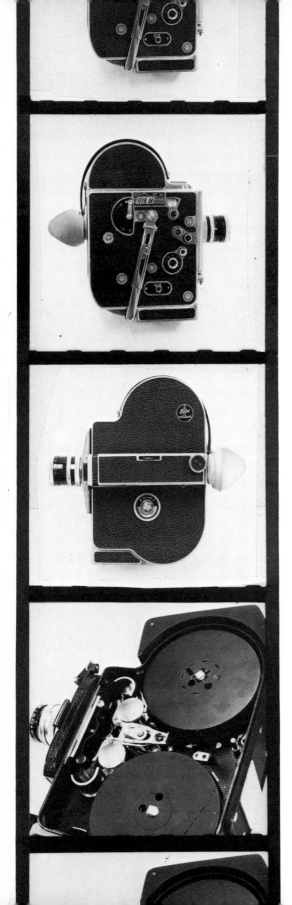

is projected is the one which ran through the camera. Most 8 mm. and Super 8 films are reversal. For initial work this is quite acceptable but for a longer film it may be advisable to use negative film. From this negative one print or cutting copy is made. The negative is then filed away and cut later to match the finely edited cutting copy exactly. *Colour* negative film is too expensive for the average film group.

THE MOVING IMAGE

A cine-film is a series of still photographs which if projected in rapid succession (16, 18, or 24 frames per second) give the illusion of movement. Each frame of film is slightly different from the one which preceded it. The illusion of movement comes about because of what is known as *persistence of vision*. If an image is shown instantaneously, the retina of the human eye will persist in seeing that image for a very short time (approximately one-tenth of a second) after it has gone. It is this phenomenon which makes cine-photography possible.

CINE-CAMERAS

All cine-cameras have certain basic points in common:
1 They are like lightproof boxes.
2 A lens with an adjustable diaphragm is fitted.
3 There is some means of transporting the film through the camera.
4 The image from the lens is focused sharply on the film.
5 A shutter mechanism enables each frame of film to be accurately exposed in turn.
6 Some form of viewfinder is attached or built in.

REFLEX AND NON-REFLEX CAMERAS

A *reflex* camera is one in which the viewfinder 'looks through' the lens of the camera. This means that focusing and size and position of image can always be accurately assessed.

A 16 mm. non-reflex camera

A *non-reflex* camera has a viewfinder which is built on to the camera but does not see directly through the lens. With this type of camera, focusing has to be done by measurement of distance.

The majority of Super 8 cameras are reflex. 8 mm. and 16 mm. cameras may be purchased in both types.

Page 13 shows an example of an 8 mm. non-reflex camera. It is clockwork and the winding mechanism may be seen on its right side. The lenses are on a movable turret. This particular turret will take three lenses, though only two are in the illustration. The semi-automatic light meter is just above the turret.

Page 13 also shows a Super 8 camera. This is a reflex camera with a built-in light meter and zoom lens. The magazine on top of the camera holds the cassette of film. The camera is battery operated which facilitates long takes. This and the previous camera are simple to operate. They are capable of many technical feats not mentioned here. It is hoped that the reader will obtain further details from a photographic dealer once he has decided the type of cine-camera he wants.

Page 14 shows three views of a 16 mm. non-reflex camera. This is a clockwork camera. The viewfinder with a rubber eyepiece is detachable. This is valuable when choosing locations or camera positions. The close-up shows the inside of the camera with a film threaded. The film is transported from the top spool to the bottom.

LENSES

The lens is the eye of the camera. As such it must be treated with the utmost care. It should not be cleaned with anything but a lens tissue. A handkerchief, however soft, should not be used. Sand, grit, or grease will not only damage any lens but may cause loss of light. This can lead to a lowering of picture brilliance when the film is projected. Extremely soft lens brushes are available

Examples of lenses

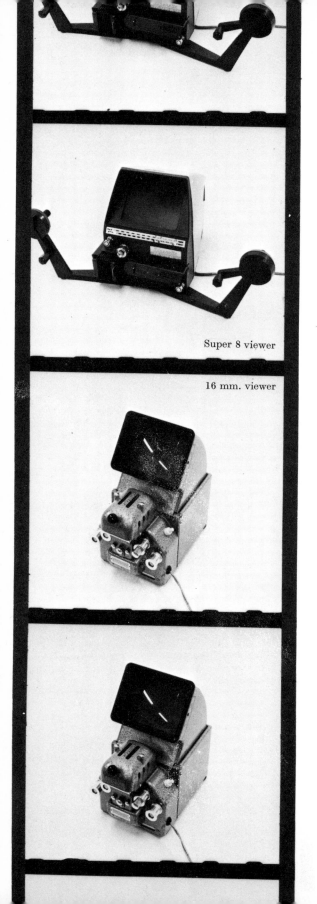

Super 8 viewer

16 mm. viewer

from photographic dealers. They are like pocket pens and therefore easy to carry. Meths. and cotton wool (or alcohol on lint-free cloth) will remove any grease or finger-marks from a lens.

TYPES OF LENSES

The close-up shot of a camera on page 15 shows the three basic lenses common to all types of film work. These are generally known as *normal* (the one on the camera), *wide angle* (the short one), and *telephoto* (the long one). The angle of vision of a lens is determined by its focal length. The shorter the focal length, the wider the angle of vision. A lens with a very long focal length acts as a telescope attached to the camera.

The pictures illustrated were all taken from approximately the same point of view using three different lenses. The smallest used a 10 mm. wide-angle lens, the largest one a 75 mm. or telephoto lens, and the middle a 25 mm. or normal lens.

With a *zoom* lens the change of focal length may be operated by a button or lever – hence the 'zoom' effect.

Useful points about lenses are:
1   A wide-angle lens gives a great depth of field as well as a wide angle of vision.
2   A telephoto lens gives a smaller depth of field with a narrow angle of vision.
3   A wide-angle lens distorts perspective. This is particularly apparent in architectural shots or big close-ups of faces.
4   A telephoto lens telescopes the effect of distance. A person walking towards the camera on telephoto appears to be going through the motions of walking without getting anywhere.
5   All lenses should be covered with a lens-cap when not in use.

FOCUSING A ZOOM LENS

All zoom lenses are reflex, which means that you can focus them by sight. Be-

16

fore focusing it is essential to zoom right in on the subject. If this is not done the subject will appear to be in focus when it is not. This is necessary when the lighting conditions are poor.

PROJECTION FACILITIES

Projectors vary a great deal in price according to their ability to 'throw' the picture a large or small distance and the quality of the lens. A good projector is a definite asset to any group. It is better to spend more money on a more powerful projector than to buy both a projector and a screen. A screen is not so essential. A flat wall or board painted with white emulsion is adequate at first. It is only for performances that extra care should be given to projection facilities. The first priority for a group should be to produce film which warrants good projection facilities.

Splices, especially on 8 mm. film will jump badly as they pass through some projectors. It is essential to test a projector with a piece of spliced film before a purchase is made.

Some projectors have zoom lenses. This enables the projectionist to control the size of the image at any given distance from the screen. This is particularly useful if the projection room is small.

EDITING EQUIPMENT

Every film group should possess at least one hand-winding viewer, a pair of rewind arms, and a splicer.

Page 16 shows a Super 8 and a 16 mm. viewer. The Super 8 viewer has winding arms attached. These fold back when not in use. The 16 mm. viewer requires separate winding arms. The picture may be wound through a viewer either backwards or forwards.

Page 17 shows a cement splicer for 16 mm. film. This type of splicer is sturdy and functional. Any equipment to be used for group filming should fulfil this requirement. It is possible to buy

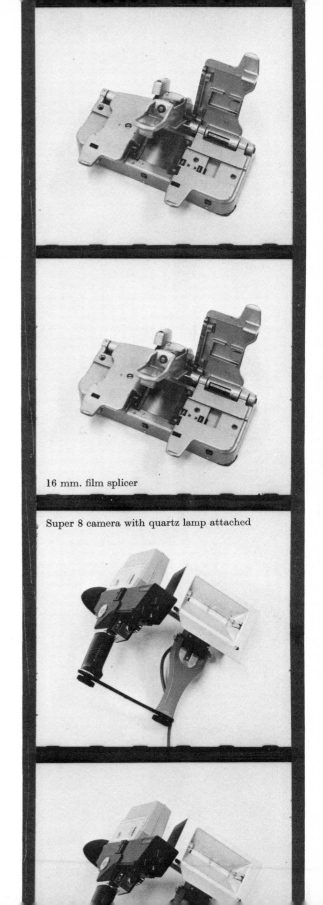

16 mm. film splicer

Super 8 camera with quartz lamp attached

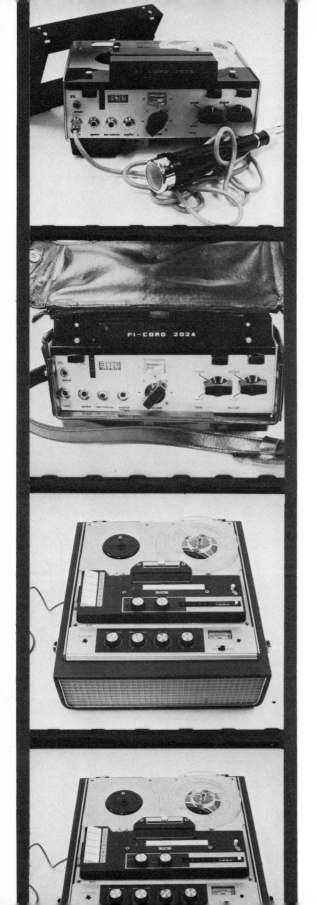

splicers which will join both 8 mm. and
16 mm. film. Note: when a cement
splice is made, the emulsion is scraped
from the end of the film. This helps the
cement to form a good joint. Some edi-
tors prefer to scrape *both* pieces of film
to be joined. This produces a strong
joint and at the same time makes the
splice thinner.

WHICH GAUGE TO WORK ON

If a group is starting from nothing it is
difficult to know which gauge of film to
choose. Each gauge has its advantages
and disadvantages. Some of these are
set out below. They may be of use in
determining your choice.

8 mm. film

Advantages: inexpensive. Available in
a variety of stocks including different
types of black-and-white film. Wider
choice and range of cameras, although
they must be purchased second-hand.

Disadvantages: it is difficult to edit
and it is not known how much longer it
will be on the market.

Super 8 film

Advantages: larger picture frame
which gives better picture throw and
quality on projection. Editing is also a
little easier.

Disadvantages: limited range of film
stock at the moment; requires all new
equipment as there has not been time
for a second-hand market to develop.

16 mm. film

Advantages: virtually a professional
gauge; great range of film stocks available; very good for editing.

Disadvantages: more expensive than
the other two gauges; two and a quarter
minutes of 16 mm. costs more than
double the amount of four minutes of
8 mm. film; 16 mm. cameras are also
expensive, especially if they are reflex.

Sound equipment

A group should be as concerned to
possess good sound recording equipment as to purchase cameras and

Relatively inexpensive tape-recorders. The one in the
leather case is portable

18

projectors. One portable and one mains (or plug-in type) tape-recorder are basic requirements. Look for sturdy equipment and avoid gimmicks. Tape-recorders take more knocks than any other film gear.

Portable tape-recorders

There are so many different tape-recorders on the market today that one can only suggest basic points to look for. Most portable tape-recorders will record speech quite well but are not so good with music. They are valuable for street interviews and gathering 'effects'.

The tape-recorder opposite is solid and contained in a leather carrying case. It will record at $3\frac{3}{4}$ or $7\frac{1}{2}$ i.p.s. Most speech is satisfactory if recorded at $3\frac{3}{4}$ i.p.s. but music should always be recorded at $7\frac{1}{2}$ i.p.s. A portable tape-recorder should be simple and quick to operate, as it is often used in circumstances where there is little time for preparation. Many portable tape-recorders, such as the one illustrated, have separate controls to start the motor and set the machine in motion. This means that it is easy for the batteries to run down although the tape-spools are not turning.

Mains (or plug-in) tape-recorders

There are three types of tape-recorders available, known as *twin-track (two-track)*, *four-track*, and *full-track (eight-track)*. The latter are mainly for professional use. On a twin-track machine the tape is run through once, then turned over and run through again. A four-track machine has two tracks on each half of the tape. For most groups a twin-track machine is ideal.

Four-track tape-recorders will record a great amount of information on one tape, but they can cause havoc if any physical cutting of tape is done during editing. This is because there are two tracks on each half of the tape and a channel switch on the recorder which picks out one of the four tracks. If any sound is on the wrong track it cannot be spliced until it has been re-recorded. Defenders of four-track machines will rightly point out that they do make it possible to superimpose one track on top of another. For a group who have just been formed they are a little too complex.

The other tape-recorder illustrated is twin-tracked, having several interesting features. It can record at three different speeds ($1\frac{7}{8}$, $3\frac{3}{4}$, and $7\frac{1}{2}$ i.p.s.). Sound from two other recorders can be mixed through the *radio* and *microphone* inputs. The *record level* indicator is large and accurate.

These features are the type to look for in a machine. Tape-recorders which set the level for a microphone automatically are often unsuitable for group work; they make experimentation difficult and there may be times when one wishes to over- or under-record sound.

Notes on sound recording:

1   Whenever possible the microphone should be placed on some kind of stand.
2   Try not to alter the level once a recording has started.
3   Always record well below overload.

No mention has been made of microphones. This is because the ones provided with a tape-recorder are quite suitable for group work. Other information on microphones may be learnt as required. For lighting equipment, see page 62.

Scripting

For many people the problems of obtaining equipment seem enormous and they usually think that once the camera has been purchased the main troubles are over. In fact they are just beginning. Sooner or later the members of any film group ask the inevitable question: 'What shall we film?' The possibilities are immense. The difficulty is to decide on one subject which is easy to handle. I suggest that a good way to begin is to think in terms of filming an *incident* rather than a *story*. This incident need only last for one reel of 8 mm. film. Allowing for a minimum amount of editing, the film will then last about three-and-a-half minutes. This approach has the advantage that it gives each member the opportunity to handle the concept of a complete short film.

Having decided on this approach, two questions arise:

1 What kind of incident?
2 What is the best way to script it?

CHOOSING AN INCIDENT

Tempting as it is to make a first film about a bank robbery, or some such fantasy as 'the day the school disappeared', these films require a great deal of preparation over a longish period of time. They are often of such a length that they use up most of the available film stock. This knowledge creates tension among all members as the time for shooting approaches. When the film is seen before editing this strain is often apparent in the movement of both actors and camera. Probably few members of the group have been really involved in the filming but, success or failure, this is all that the group will be able to afford to do unless they obtain more money.

Therefore, I recommend that beginners should start with a series of shorter films. Moreover, a film with a long and intricate or poorly thought out plot, is more likely to condemn itself to failure from the outset than a short one. Any doubts tend to be rationalized away by saying that a film must be made at all costs, but this approach destroys enthusiasm once the group is aware that things are not going well. Almost anything seems like a good idea when a group is eager to start working; two weeks later the idea can be seen for what it is. There must be a large number of 8 mm. cine-cameras hidden away in cupboards by people who once had the idea of forming a film group. A high percentage of films are never finished and when they are shown they are prefaced by a ten minute justification of what is about to be seen; more humble beginnings often produce much more satisfying results.

Keep the incident to be filmed simple requiring little or no set building or special props. The best place to begin is in a room or in the street where countless simple incidents occur every day. Members should learn to become aware of the world around them. It is astute observation which produces film just as much as mere enthusiasm. Sometimes a film may be based on an observed incident, sometimes on an imaginary one. It is often better to adapt the truth rather than invent something purely from the imagination. The following is an example of an observed incident which was written in a notebook later in the day.

An elderly woman is standing at a bus-stop. After about a minute a man walks up. He is short and thickset. He carries a small suitcase. His hair is too long and very greasy. He is pale and looks angry. About eight yards behind him a woman walks towards the stop. She is dressed in a nondescript coat which she holds near to her body to keep warm. On her feet she wears old fluffy slippers. Her hair is in curlers. She talks to the man in a strong local accent:

WOMAN: Come on back. Just to talk. You can't go off now. I just want to talk, that's all. Come back with me.

MAN: No! (*He then swears profusely in a manner which is impossible to understand.*)

The woman comes close to the man while this is happening. They exchange dark looks and some kind of sinister but silent communication takes place.

WOMAN (*stepping back suddenly*): Alright! If that's the way you feel it doesn't worry me. You just go on and do it if you want. . . .

The bus-stop sequence

Her talk becomes garbled sound. She walks about 10 yards up the road and stops by a small wall, looking hard at the man. He stays at the stop staring across the road for a couple of minutes. Then quite suddenly he turns and walks towards the woman. He is still swearing though it is difficult to pick out any of the words. The woman sees him coming and walks towards him.

WOMAN: That's right. Come on. I'm not annoyed. I just want to talk, that's all.

They meet and walk up the road. The woman links her arm through the man's. About twenty yards up the road they enter a house. Two minutes later the man returns, stands at the bus-stop and rides away on the next bus.

The main point to notice here, aside from what actually happens, is the *way* it has been recorded. By deliberately trying to remember things in chronological order, the beginnings of a script are inevitable. There has been no need to search for an idea or a story. For some people, what has been written would provide an adequate shooting script. This brings us to a consideration of the ways in which a script may be put on paper.

The bus-stop sequence (cont.)

'I for one have no patience with the growing method of having every camera shot sketched beforehand so that the director, camera-man, and actors can work by rote. It destroys that spontaneity of feeling which is the essence of film art; though of course many films are so unimportant that it does not matter how they are shot: they never were alive at any moment.' (Dudley Nichols.)

WRITING A SCRIPT

The incident at the bus-stop is only one of hundreds that group members will have observed. These incidents demand exacting powers of observation so that every relevant detail of the scene is absorbed, even the most minute fleeting expression in the eyes – *observation is not something which belongs solely to the professional film-maker*. Once an incident has been recorded, thought must be given to the different ways in which it may be filmed. The original incident may be slightly adapted for reasons of location or practicality.

There is no right way to write a script. There are, however, a number of different approaches which have been proved successful by commercial directors or members of film groups. Basically these are four in number:

The breakdown script
In this type of scripting the length of shot is given in seconds (in the profession it is normal to work in feet). It is interesting that a television script has come to resemble this traditional type of film script, while many film directors have moved to a much freer approach.

The prose script
A piece of 'cine-writing', though it rarely includes much technical terminology.

The storyboard script
This is of value if one has extreme clarity of ideas and powers of visualization; also if one is muddle-headed and cannot visualize anything unless it is down on paper. Most film-makers find themselves somewhat between these two poles.

The 'note' script
Usually made up of jottings, not necessarily in any special order. This approach is inadvisable without some previous filming experience.

In order to give some clarity to the various forms of scripting, the incident observed at the bus-stop will be set out in each of the four ways mentioned.

The breakdown script

SCENE 1 SHOT 1
Time (or footage)   Ten seconds.
Long shot   Bus-stop. Two or three people in queue. Man carrying suitcase joins queue and stands facing camera, though not looking into it.

SCENE 1   SHOT 2
Time   Four seconds.
Close-up   Man's face from front. Annoyed. His eyes move
                  from side to side.

SCENE 1   SHOT 3
Time   Ten seconds.
Long shot   As for shot 1. After three seconds, camera pans to
                  right and picks up woman in old coat. She is talking
                  to the man.

SCENE 1   SHOT 4
Time   Five seconds.
Medium shot   The woman has walked closer and they are both in
                  the frame. She lifts her hand from her side slightly
                  – beckoning.

SCENE 1   SHOT 5
Time   Three seconds.
Close-up   Man's face as he scowls and turns towards the
                  woman.

SCENE 1   SHOT 6
Time   Six seconds.
Medium shot   From behind man's shoulder, looking over at
                  woman. She still talks to him.

SCENE 1   SHOT 7
Time   Twelve seconds.
Medium shot   180 degrees round behind woman. She gives up
                  talking to man, turns and walks towards the
                  camera which pulls back.

From this rigid script, the director translates what is on paper into
the language of film. The language in this case is preconceived and
can lead to stylized and formal filming and acting; for instance,
shots 3, 4, and 5 have a predictability about them which suggests
that they could look clumsy when viewed. When an inexperienced
member of a film group is directing a film under pressure, it is easy
for him to forget that he is dealing with people. This is unfortunate
and coupled with the kind of script we have just seen, can lead to
comments such as: 'When I shout "Action!" Fred – you scowl for
four seconds. O.K.?' Fred scowls in exaggerated fashion. Films made
in this way seldom satisfy even the mildly critical. If, however, he can
always remain aware of his team as individuals, he will gain both their
respect and a responsive performance.

The prose script
The bus-stop can be seen from across the road. There are a few people
waiting in the queue.
    A man carrying a suitcase walks up and joins the queue. He looks

very annoyed and appears to be muttering to himself as he turns towards us.

A few yards behind there is a woman who is speaking loudly to him. She is agitated. Her coat and old fluffy slippers, along with the curlers in her hair, make her look incongruous and rather grotesque.

The man makes no reply to her verbal and visual beckonings. She walks away up the road.

This is brief and has no technical terminology about the manner of filming. The director is left to decide how to set about his work and the stress is on the characters rather than the language of film. From a belief in the characters and a wish to film them, a language of film can grow in its own good time. For those interested *Last Year in Marienbad*, written as a cine-novel, is a first-class example of this type of scripting (see bibliography).

The storyboard script
Although some of us naturally think in terms of images and therefore require to adopt the storyboard technique, others, especially those with an ability to draw, prefer to draw in them as well. It is inadvisable to ask members of a film group to draw a storyboard which results in complete disillusionment because they have not picked up a pencil for years.

In the field of advertising there are 'visualizers', whose job is to show a client how a finished film will look. There is a strong case for the work they do. However, a film group is not quite the same; a member should not rely too strongly on this approach. If this method of scripting is used it should be kept simple and the separate drawings should be working drawings rather than finished pictures (page 26). A few simple notes should accompany each drawing:

1   From across road. Bus-stop near left-hand side of frame.
2   Profile set also on left-hand side of frame.
3   This shows positioning of characters at the end of shot.
4   Note the amount of coverage given to the length of the figures.
5   Face moves from front to side view.
6   This may include others in the queue to build out the composition.

The 'note' script
Bus-stop – queue.
    Woman/man – conflict.
    Watch for her gestures. Don't let her act.
    Man seen more in close-up.
    Watch his pace when he walks.
    When she leaves his face must stay blank – no mouth-opening gestures.

This kind of script is more personal. The concept of the film is so firmly rooted in the director's mind that he is now solely concerned with particular *aspects* of the film in relation to the *whole*. If this approach is used well it can produce good film. A group member, however, should never be tempted to use this method as a way out of any serious thought; it is the result of serious thought. For this

Storyboard script

reason I suggest that you do not attempt to use it until you have gained a certain amount of experience. The note script should not be confused with making notes. Almost everyone makes notes, but few of us can finish a script in note form.

Any method of scripting has its own assets and defects. What is important is that the group choose the most suitable method for themselves in any given film. To be successful a film group must be adaptable. The methods of scripting are suggested here almost as preliminary exercises. As any group gains more experience, they should no longer find it necessary to think about *how* to script. But for the beginner without experience I would strongly recommend the prose script approach to start with.

Another point mentioned earlier is that film language is something to be learnt by discovery not by rote. It is better that mistakes be made and *discovered* in relation to a particular film. You can afford to learn this way if initial exercises are on one reel of 8 mm. film. You will soon realize that what is a mistake in one place may be just what is needed in another. Rules are either learnt in order that they may be broken or built up into a new set of rules and adapted according to experience.

No mention has been made previously of the kind of story that a group should aim at filming after gaining some experience. This is because it is not always *necessary* to think in terms of films with stories, although it is true that film has tended to follow a literary path. Story or plot were once of prime importance and everything else was subservient. This story was a sequence of events which followed a preconceived order to a preordained end. Since the turn of the century, both literature and drama have shifted their emphasis away from the content of the plot. Film groups must constantly ask themselves what *they* mean by a story. It has been suggested that many group-made films fall down because of the kind of story or plot they employ. I suggest that instead of choosing the adventure or 'whodunnit' type where the main emphasis is usually on the 'and then . . . and then . . . and then', perhaps they would be wiser to re-place this constant asking 'What happens next?' by 'What happens?'

More and more commercial film-makers are questioning the value of a narrative plot and beginning to search for other abstract values and themes. Film groups, too, can look beyond the mere spinning of a filmic yarn. Even directors of westerns and adventure films are changing their approach. In some of his films Howard Hawks takes on a grand scale what could be described as an incident; this is particularly true of *Rio Bravo* and *El Dorado*.

'I also decided that audiences were getting tired of plots. . . . And so far it has worked out very well. People seem to like it better. I don't mean that if a story comes along you shouldn't do it, but I think the average plot is pretty time worn. Television has come in and they have used so many thousands of plots that people are getting tired of them. They're a little too inclined – if you lay a plot down – to say, "Oh, I've seen this before". But if you can keep them from knowing what the plot is you have a chance of holding their interest. And it leads to characters – so that you may write what the character might think and the character motivates your story and the situations – and it's when a character believes in something that a situation happens, not because you write it to happen.' (Howard Hawks.)

There is, however, always place for a film which tells a really good story. Some directors spend all their time searching for one. But others, from both Hollywood and the European cinema, prefer to look for characters which are so authentic that the film evolves around them. Do not start off with a story film before giving serious consideration to other possibilities.

Look first to your immediate surroundings for inspiration – to friends and the people who live in your district. Exaggerated dramatic caricature should be avoided when scripting a film. It is better to aim at sincerity of approach rather than dramatic superficiality or slickness.

This book does not deal specifically with *documentary* film-making but the approach suggested here may be termed 'dramatic documentary'. Its aim is to encourage film groups to *look at, then comment on* aspects of life as they see it. This should be of prime importance, whichever method of scripting one chooses.

Shooting

'The time cannot long be delayed when technical changes will alter the whole balance of the movies. Already machines exist which are able to tape-record both sound and vision in "natural" conditions. As soon as these machines become commonplace (and I doubt whether it will take very long), it will be possible to create films without the ponderous paraphernalia of studio equipment and staff which have so far made the imagination of the film-makers subject, except in exceptional circumstances, to the exigencies of the budget makers and the supposed demands of the mass audience.' (Frederic Raphael.)

Film equipment is changing and progressing so fast that new products are constantly appearing on the market. Film groups can, therefore, be sure that as time goes on they need worry less and less about technical matters. For some this is a disappointment. There are those in film groups who are more interested in equipment than in making films and love to boast that their camera is reflex and their zoom lens power operated. A knowledge of technical matters is certainly an asset and for any aspiring professional a necessity, but it should facilitate, not dominate the work of a film group. Many cine enthusiasts tend to hide behind their technical knowledge. They can tell you where to buy the latest model monopod or pre-shot titles, but what they need to do is to think in terms of making a statement on film.

Within the film industries of the world there are many people experimenting and fighting to rid themselves of outmoded methods of working. Film-makers (movie-makers) are beginning to work successfully on 16 mm. A team of two people can now shoot a synchronous sound film without much discomfort. A team of four can manage with ease in normal light conditions. This new freedom enables them to discover more fully the potential of the medium, for the restrictions they have to face are now self-imposed. This cuts short a lot of time-wasting procedure.

There is a certain basic procedure common to any method of shooting. This is in the time of preparation. It is not often that the group will go out without the camera, but it has been known. In order to overcome these difficulties you should have a check-list. This will show exactly what equipment is required for the shooting, including the type and amount of film stock to be used, light meter, tripod, camera, and any special accessories. One member of the group should be responsible for this job and should have the list pinned on a board which he carries. It must be stressed that this member will not be expected to do the same job *every time*. As experience is gained, these jobs should become interchangeable. When initial film exercises are being carried out, this may well happen, especially if these exercises are short. Always take the shooting script, whatever form it may have. It saves much bad feeling and time.

Whichever method of shooting you employ, there are certain points to be considered when using the camera; they may be extremely obvious, but nevertheless they are worth stating. They are not concerned with 'language' of film, but with obtaining the kind of pictures you want.

1 Make sure the camera is properly loaded. If it is a non-reflex camera be certain to remove the lens-cap before shooting.
2 If there is not an automatic light meter in the camera, be sure to set the correct aperture (*f*-stop).
3 If the camera is non-reflex do not forget to focus it.
4 If you are hand holding the camera, hold it as steady as possible.
5 When panning (to move the camera across from one side of the scene to the other move the camera very slowly. Always bring the camera to rest at the end of a pan.
6 Do not use a zoom lens when hand holding a camera.
7 Watch the footage counter to make sure you still have film left.
8 If it is clockwork, rewind the camera after every shot.
9 Vary the camera angle when approaching a subject. A zigzag approach is a good idea.
10 Think more about *what* you are trying to film rather than if it 'looks good'.

These ten points will at least help the pictures to be recognizable and clear, irrespective of the kind of film being made. Most groups stumble over these points when they begin. Such things as the speed at which you pan, for instance, can only be learnt by experience. Constant use of the zoom lens can prove extremely nauseating. On the whole it is better to be as simple as possible in approach. Indeed, the best results are often obtained on the simplest cameras. When using a fixed-lens camera for a close-up shot, go in close; for a long shot move far away. This *physical* involvement in shooting is a great help in understanding the medium. It also gives other members of the group a clear indication of what is going on.

I suggest that you should shoot film in sequence when beginning. This forces you to think in *filmic* terms; otherwise it is easy to find that one aspect of the film dominates at the expense of another. This method means limiting yourself to a single location. For the purposes of this chapter, this limitation will apply. It will also be assumed that the film shot is only one reel in length and will be shot in sequence.

There are two basic approaches to shooting a film: *rigid* and *free*. Once again a compromise is often the answer for most groups. The easiest way to explain these approaches is by setting out examples of both. Give yourself the opportunity of using both methods and decide which you find most suitable. An incident is given once more as the basis for working. Part of this incident will be written out as a script in each case and the method of working described.

THE INCIDENT

A girl is standing outside a laundrette (laundromat). She has a bag of washing. A boy walks up to the building, also carrying some washing. They appear to know each other and go inside together. We see them do their washing in two machines, read magazines and soap-powder boxes. During this time they do not speak to each other, though they are sitting side by side. When the washing has been dried, they pack up their bags and leave together. When they are outside they nod to each other and walk away in opposite directions.

The boy and girl enter the laundrette (laundromat)

31

RIGID SHOOTING

Sample script

SCENE 1   SHOT 1
Time: nine seconds
Medium long shot: Girl standing out-
  side laundrette (laundromat).

SCENE 1   SHOT 2
Time: four seconds
Medium shot: From beside the girl. Boy
  can be seen walking towards her.

SCENE 1   SHOT 3
Time: six seconds
Long shot: They meet and nod to each
  other, then enter laundrette (laundromat). Cut to

SCENE 2   SHOT 1
Time: ten seconds
Medium shot: From inside the laundrette (laundromat) as they walk to
  the machines, etc., etc., etc.

This is something of the kind of
script which would be used to shoot to
a rigid pattern using a director. Starting outside the laundrette the camera is
set up and the girl positioned. In order
to let her know when shooting is to
begin, the director shouts 'Action' and
then the camera is kept running for
exactly ten seconds.

One or two members operate the
camera. The director is there to co-
ordinate the movements of actors and
camera and keep a strict eye on the
length of shots. 'Action' and 'Cut' become the dominant words. Ensure that
the action starts just *before* the camera
when working in this way. Remember
that much of the editing is being done
in the camera.

FREE SHOOTING

Sample script

1 Outside the laundrette (laundromat).
   The girl waits.
2 Boy approaches.
3 Into laundrette (laundromat).
4 From inside. We see them enter.

Inside the laundrette (laundromat)

32

The script is not at all technical. There is no mention of the length or type of shot to be obtained. A director is unnecessary for the cameraman *is* the director. This disposes of endless chatter about what the director 'wants' from his actors and technicians. The cameraman is the person who wishes to make a film of this particular incident. The only information he needs to communicate is to his two characters. The work, therefore, is personal and relaxed. It must be stressed that a film exercise such as this can easily be shot in a couple of hours. Therefore, the following week there should be a different cameraman, different actors, and a fresh subject. In this way no member of a group keeps one job, so that over a period of six months each member of the group should have had experience both in front of and behind the camera.

A word should be said about the cameraman's approach to this kind of shooting. For the opening shot he is more likely to ask the girl to stand outside the building and just 'wait', rather than shout 'Action'. When he had filmed her waiting, he would come and tell her so. Later in the film, where they are both seated side by side, he would also film in quite a free manner. Instead of thinking in terms of static shots, the cameraman is thinking in terms of what he can *see* in relation to what he is trying to *say*. This establishes a more natural atmosphere and avoids setting up a carefully composed, beautifully exposed shot which portrays the characters as dummies. There are no cries of 'Action'; the actors just ignore the camera, whether it is close to their heads or far-away from them. The cameraman will tell them what is happening, he may even talk them through each shot as he shoots it.

Laundrette (laundromat) sequence (cont.)

33

For groups who find either of these methods of shooting too extreme, the answer is for the cameraman to have a shooting script in his pocket. This shooting script would be comparatively non-technical, telling him the length of each shot and occasionally specifying the type of shot. The script stays in his pocket and it is only referred to if he gets stuck. If the cameraman is filming an incident of his own choice, he seldom forgets what he is doing. He will have thought about it so much that he begins to see the film in his head as he is shooting. The length of each shot will no longer depend on a sheet of paper but on what he can see. The shooting is flexible. If a close-up shot was scripted to last twenty seconds and he can see that it is boring, he will stop the camera. This will ensure a lively, human element in the filming.

WHY SHOOT IN CHRONOLOGICAL ORDER?

Film is full of paradoxes; for instance, it is easier to grasp the salient points of editing by shooting film as though it were already edited. This self-discipline, far from being inhibiting, can bring a new freshness to the film. It does not require a great deal of experience to judge when to stop and start the camera. In the laundrette (laundromat) incident the action can be carefully timed so that it flows easily when the couple go inside. Learn to watch carefully to see the point at which the camera stops running. When changing angle it is then possible to pick up that particular action at the precise point at which it was left. Remember that this method requires the action to begin *before* the camera. The repetition of the same action for shooting will be discussed in relation to film acting (page 49).

This is an excellent way of beginning as it has the advantage that each group member has the chance to try every job. The examples quoted here usually involve about half a dozen people.

If you find this way of working somewhat unusual, it is probably because you have certain preconceptions about film-making. Start with an open mind and you will find you can produce very satisfying results. These results will need no special justification and will not be naïve or superficial even though initial exercises may be only four minutes in length. If you wish to write, you have to learn to look and listen before beginning a novel. With filming you have to find out just what a cine-camera will do. Aim at shooting a variety of subjects over a period of months, giving every member a chance to handle the camera. The commercial distinctions of jobs are no longer necessary in film groups. In a group all jobs, including acting, should be interchangeable. Although some members will find they prefer to be an 'actor' or a 'cameraman', the essential point is that the group is a *group* of *film-makers*.

In general this method involves few group members. If the group is a large one, remember that these films can be made at the rate of one a week without too much effort so that, while some group members are out shooting, others can be preparing another film. (Remember, that enthusiasm flags if members are not kept fully occupied.) This whole process then becomes cyclical and a group may be working

Far distant	FD	Long shot	LS	Mid shot	MS
Mid distant	MD	Mid shot	MS	Close-up	CU
Near distant	ND	Near shot	NS	Big close-up	BCU

Types of shots and suggested abbreviations

on two or three films at once. The films being made are within the group's powers to handle efficiently. Whether a group intends to concentrate on short films or go on to story films or documentaries, this approach is equally valid. The method of shooting can be the same for a half-hour story film as for a four-minute incident. If shooting takes place in several different locations, each session approximates in length to a four-minute film.

35

Once a group has been in existence long enough for every member to have shot some film, the future general policy of the group must be decided. Some groups find that shooting film in the way suggested here, plus the addition of sound-tracks, provides them with a permanent approach to film-making. The length of their films will grow but these films will always be statements based on personal experience. Naturally, the method of shooting will vary from member to member. One of the main aims of working in this way is to allow group members to come to terms with film in their own time and at their own level.

The group should treat film-making as a creative activity that is a little more than merely an agreeable way of passing time, otherwise the cry is always 'How do you script? How do you shoot film?' This kind of questioning is usually seeking the easiest way to obtain a slick result. However, there is no easy formula to produce a slick result. Moreover, a film which has been shot to a series of cast-iron rules is often very dead, akin to the work of the young painter who is more concerned with which style he uses rather than what he paints. Style should be discovered in retrospect.

The main point to remember when shooting film is that it is a time of *looking* and *observing*, then *recording*. If what is recorded is bad, then the film will be bad. If the placing and actions of the characters is false, the film will be false. If, on the other hand, what is recorded is good, the film will be good.

Editing

Editing is the next most important and formative facet of film-making. It is the process which determines the tempo and flow of a film and tells the audience when and what it will see and hear. First it is important to come to some understanding of what editing has meant in the past and the possibilities of its use now.

Since the beginnings of film a language of editing has grown up. This language has gradually become accepted by the cinema-going public as well as cine-enthusiasts. It is learnt and accepted with very little conscious effort. Children who watch television spy series are often ready to accept more recent developments in editing which involve jump cuts and unexplained changes of location. But the former, more established technique of editing which may be called 'academic' will be discussed first.

ACADEMIC EDITING

This type of editing is best examined in relation to a rigidly shot script. When the rushes (film straight from the camera) have been viewed, they are cut into separate shots and labelled. A record is made of the content of each shot. The film is then hung in an editing bin or some suitable dust-free container. The end of each shot is numbered with a chinagraph pencil for easy identification. Any unusable material is discarded at this stage. Nothing is kept which is fogged or poorly exposed.

The next thing the editor has to do is to assemble all the shots in order according to the shooting script. No shot is shortened at this stage, which is known as the *assembly*. When each sequence has been viewed several times, the editor begins to cut each shot to its final length. This stage is known as the *fine-cut*. For the average film group the fine-cut is the finished film. This approach to editing has been summarized by Alfred Hitchcock: 'I know it is said sometimes that a director ought to edit his own pictures if he wants to control their final form, for it is in the editing, according to this view, that a film is really brought into being. But if the scenario is planned out in detail and followed closely during production, editing should be easy. All that has to be done is to cut away irrelevancies and see that the finished film is an accurate rendering of the scenario.' This method of editing is a logical process and most film groups are happier to work in this way when they begin. One now comes back to the point of editing in the camera. Some groups feel *obliged* to shoot a film so that it can be edited afterwards. The main justification for this has been that film is *usually* edited on the bench. But if film is edited as it is shot, the work done on the bench will only involve cutting out leader and blank film and splicing together sequences which have been shot at different locations. This overcomes the long time lapse between shooting and the actual group viewing of the final film. The viewing of the final film then becomes not a treat but a regular occurrence.

A film can look awkward at the beginning and end of each shot even after editing. This is because the young editor can become 'blind' to a rather contrived action which has been started *after* the camera begins to run. If the camera catches the action while it is happening, a swifter, smoother flow of picture is more easily obtained. There may be times when it is absolutely essential to shoot shots with a gap between them, but these are rare. More will be said about editing in the camera when the language of academic editing has been examined a little more closely. To do this we shall examine a specific sequence in relation to the way it may be edited, both on the bench and in the camera. The illustrations show each cut in the action.

Summary of sequence to be edited

A man and a woman are in a room together. The woman is seated and the man is standing. They are having a conversation which is interrupted by the telephone ringing. The man answers the telephone. It is a wrong number. He replaces the receiver and returns to his former position. Their conversation continues:

1 We see the man and the woman together from across the room. This is known as the *establishing* shot.
2 Cut to a close-up of them talking, seen from the same angle.
3 Cut to extreme close-up of telephone (we assume it is ringing).
4 Cut to close-up of man's face.
5 Cut to 'two shot' which includes the phone. Man walks to it immediately.
6–7 Cut on action as the man's hand picks up the receiver. Follow it up to his ear.
8 He puts the receiver down in medium shot.
9 Cut on action to his hand on the telephone.
10 Cut to long shot. The man walks back to his original position and turns round to face woman. Cut on action to:
11 Close-up of man's face.
12 As for shot 2.

If this sequence is shot to a rigid script, each shot will be clearly marked out and planned. The action will be stopped between each shot, while the camera is set up in its new position. When there is some movement as in shot 5, the camera will start first, then the man will walk to the phone. It will be the editor's job to eliminate any break or delay in the flow of action.

The sequence follows a clear pattern. The opening shot is designed to show the situation which is being filmed from far enough back to 'establish' the action. We then move in a little closer to observe the two characters. This gives density to the shots. When our attention needs to be drawn to a specific object, we see that object – the telephone.

To establish that the man has heard the telephone ringing, we are provided with a close-up of his face, etc., etc., etc. The film begins to flow with a simple and clear language of cutting. Shots 8 and 9 are particularly important. They illustrate what is known as 'cutting on the action'. In this particular instance it means that when we see the man replacing the receiver in medium shot, then we move closer to see the hand moving on to the phone, there is no jump or delay in the action. This aspect of editing is particularly helpful for making a film flow smoothly.

EDITING IN THE CAMERA

There is nothing in the previous sequence that could not have been shot in order in the camera. The approach to this method of shooting/editing would be just as clear and logical, except that the action would always start *before* the camera. The cameraman must have a clear conception of what he wishes to achieve, rather than follow a rigid script shot by shot. Cutting on the action in the camera is not as difficult as might be imagined. It can be learnt quickly. The cameraman knows when he stopped the camera. *He* asks the actors to repeat the action immediately and picks it up where he left off. This does away with a director and brings the cameraman much closer to the content and style of the action.

This method of working does not deny the validity of editing on the bench. In practice certain shots need to be trimmed, but it is not necessary to shoot film *deliberately* so that it needs to be edited afterwards. Editing in the camera also has the advantage that it takes far less time. Groups often have very limited time in which to work.

The academic editing sequence

This is particularly true of film work done within the school time-table.

If a film group is not too large, and if it is certain that it will be working over a considerable period of time, each member of the group can gain experience in this way of working. All members of the group should have a thorough understanding of what film will and will not do for them. This should be done in the quickest possible time and editing in the camera is one way to provide this experience. When this has been accomplished there is a strong case for editing on the bench.

EDITING ON THE BENCH

There are certain visually powerful and creative elements which demand that the film be edited after it has been shot.

When the editor sits down with a simple hand-winding viewer, he should always remember that editing should be helpful to the film. It is a positive procedure and should not be imposed unless it is necessary. On first discovering what it means to cut on action, it is tempting to use this technique over and over again. This is also true of quick cutting or the use of cutaways (see page 41). When a film has been edited satisfactorily, the editing should not attract attention. Film is a composite medium; if any one element – be it editing, the quality of the images, or the use of sound – predominates, then something is wrong. In order to *discuss* film, these elements have been studied separately, but finally it is the film as a whole that counts.

Editing sequence (cont.)

INTERCUTTING

Intercutting is usually carried out on the editing bench. This process enables us to see the action from a completely different viewpoint or location. For example, a piece of film shows postmen at work on a mail train. We see them sorting the mail as the train moves along with lights flashing past outside. Then a shot is *intercut* which is taken from a crossing as the train thunders past. This type of cut enriches the content of a film by showing it from another viewpoint.

Or again, it may be that this particular film aims at showing how the train will arrive at its final destination at the same time as a mail van which is driving to the station to pick up the mail: we see the train going along then the mail van driving along deserted roads, then a flash back to the train. Although we are seeing different locations, inter-cutting suggests that what is happening is all happening *at the same time*.

On a more humble level, the same process of intercutting may be used to show two young people on their way to a show. One of them may be travelling in a bus, the other by tube (subway) or on foot.

The use of the cutaway

The cutaway shot is what it suggests – a shot which cuts away from a subject and back to it again. It can serve several purposes. Imagine a scene where a couple are walking down the road looking in shop windows. If we wish to *extend* the time it takes them to walk past four shops, we cut away from them walking, to look at a general view of the shops, then back to the couple at the exact point of action where they were left. Repeat this once or twice and their walk is extended in time. This also works in reverse. If they are walking down a long road and we wish to shorten the time it takes, cutaway shots may be inserted. Each time we cut back to the couple they are considerably farther down the road, but the jump has not been visually uncomfortable.

A cutaway is also useful if there is a mistake in the middle of a shot. This may be due to fogged film or a character walking out of focus or out of frame.

Editing to create a mood

The general mood of a film can be influenced by the way it is edited. This may be done by varying the speed of cutting from one shot to another. The editor should gauge the length of the shot by what the film is trying to say. If the film is concerned with some aspect of rural life, the pace of cutting will probably be slower than a film illustrating the rush hour in a city. There is no law which determines the length of shots. Common sense is the best guide. Excitement can be built up by the gradual quickening of tempo when cutting. Boredom or exhaustion require the use of much longer shots. Tension in a scene will grow if big close-ups of eyes or mouths speaking are cut against general conversational shots. Try to invent exercises which explore these possibilities. Over-dramatization is justified in this case.

41

OPTICALS

Opticals are used in film to join two related sequences and may denote the passing of time. The most common opticals are dissolves and fades. These are used when it is passing from one location to another without any feeling of haste, whether or not this involves a time lapse. There are other forms of opticals such as the wipe, which pushes one picture across the screen to reveal another in its place.

In the film industry opticals are done by the laboratories. All the editor has to do is to mark up the film in the required place. Another person, known as the negative cutter will cut the negative to the instructions of the editor. The laboratories will then produce the desired effect. This is somewhat of an oversimplification, but it does show that opticals take time to produce.

For the average film group, opticals will have to be done in the camera. Many 8 mm. and 16 mm. cine-cameras have a special rewind device which makes a dissolve possible. A fade-in or a fade-out may be achieved by opening or closing the aperture of the lens to the correct f-stop (Shooting, page 29). Generally speaking, opticals like zoom shots, should be used sparingly and with care. They lead to an approach to film-making which is akin to falling in love with the camera. It takes considerable time and experience to achieve anything more than a fade; the fade-in and fade-out are the most practical and useful opticals which a group need.

THE JUMP CUT

A jump cut comes about when the transition from one shot to another does not change angle or distance sufficiently. It has been mentioned earlier that a zigzag approach to a subject ensures sufficient change in camera angle. If there is not sufficient change in distance, the subject appears literally to jump backwards or forwards on the screen. This occurs if the cameraman has finished one shot, then moved very slightly closer or farther away from the subject *without a change in camera angle*.

This kind of jump cut should not be confused with certain recent developments in editing technique. It is now quite acceptable to jump from one location to another or to condense time simply by the use of *cutting*. There is nothing illogical in this way of working. It is best illustrated by an example.

Imagine a sequence where a man has taken a girl-friend to the theatre. He discovers that he has left the tickets at home and has to rush back to get them. This could be edited with the use of dissolves, wipes, and fades in order to show the passage of time and the man's anxiety. It is also possible to show what happens by a series of straight cuts:

Shot 1   Man discovers that he has left the tickets at home and says that he will return for them.
Shot 2   Man running into tube (subway).
Shot 3   Paying for his fare.
Shot 4   Sitting in the train.

Shot 5   Hurrying from the station.
Shot 6   Entering the front gate of his house.
Shot 7   Snatching the theatre tickets from a table.
Shot 8   Leaving his house.
Shot 9   On the train again.
Shot 10 Hurrying from the train.
Shot 11 Rushing out of the station.
Shot 12 Entering the foyer of the theatre.

This approach to editing means working on the bench. The process of editing this sequence gives the editor something more to do than string together shots according to a rigid script. It is an exciting way of working. Although this example is one which condenses time, the same method can be employed in a film which moves at a slower pace.

If you are content to start by making simple short films, you will soon discover the kind of editing which is best suited to any specific film. In the past editing has followed a rigid pattern because films have been based on some kind of literary footing. That is to say, they have tried to tell a story in much the same way as a novel used to tell a story. Hence we find the sequence of a clock dissolving to another clock to denote the passing of time or perhaps the leaves of a calendar being removed one by one. If the main concern is not merely to re-count a story, but to explore certain incidents or characteristics of behaviour, the film becomes more alive and the editing more flexible.

One of the commonest mistakes when beginning to edit is to treat the audience as though it were stupid. This is usually done by over-emphasis. For example, if we are about to see a couple on the beach, we are shown a signpost which says 'To the beach'. With dramatic situations the treatment is often worse. The trouble may have started with caricature acting. The editor then ensures that the film looks false by overstating every dramatic innuendo. A man sees someone he knows in the street. We see him stop and wave in long shot. We then cut to a close-up in which he is still waving, with his eyebrows raised and grinning wildly. This is what may be termed 'caricature' editing and is unnecessary. It may even be said that people today are ready to accept the subtlest forms of visual imagery.

A final word should be said on the handling of film. Always handle film by its edges. Grease from the fingers quickly acts as an adhesive for dust. Many group films have no negatives, so it is worth a little care to preserve the quality of picture.

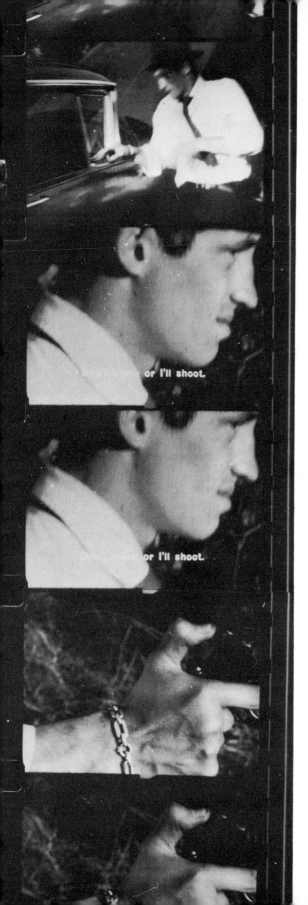

EDITING SEQUENCE

The sequence illustrated here is from a film called *Breathless* (*A Bout de Souffle*) made in 1959 and directed by Jean-Luc Godard. During the sequence Michel, in the white shirt, kills a gendarme, escapes, and makes his way back to Paris.

The editing of picture and sound is brilliantly handled, although many traditional editing rules are broken.

As the gendarme approaches, Michel reaches for his pistol which is in the car. The next shot shows a close-up profile of Michel's face. We did not see him take the pistol out of the car, but are expected to realize that he has done so. The camera moves slowly downwards and along his arm until we see the pistol. He cocks it and we move slowly along to the end of the barrel. When the shot is fired we cut instantly to the falling gendarme, but only for the length of time it takes him to fall.

The next shot shows Michel running across a field to make his getaway. Note the use of sound: from the time when the gendarme approaches until the shot is fired, there are only natural sounds on the sound-track. As soon as Michel begins to run a brassy orchestra builds up to a crescendo. This blends into a more relaxed tempo as we see the streets of Paris passing.

This type of editing leaves in only what the director considers essential information. Jump cuts and swift changes in location are accepted as part of his language. Tension is built up by the use of slow panning shots while the figures are static, leading to a tumultuous burst of music as Michel runs away. The casual quality of the murder is emphasized by the attractive music which accompanies the shots of Paris.

Sequence from *Breathless* (*A Bout de Souffle*), 1959

Acting

Most film groups devote far too little of their time to acting on the screen. Emphasis is put on scripting and shooting techniques and the performance of any character is often discussed for the first time immediately before the final take. This is strange since any piece of film, however serious or trivial, relies for its impact upon the presentation and portrayal of the characters taking part. The tension and excitement which accompanies shooting often results in a strained performance, or creates the feeling that the characters are about to break into laughter. As much serious consideration should be given to these problems as to avoiding exaggerated over-acting.

Dramatic experimentation or improvisation should be as much a part of any film group's work as any other aspect of film-making. If a group has just been formed, they can enjoyably and profitably spend three months of their time discovering their own potentialities and limitations in this field. Experiment with a series of exercises, based on dramatic improvisation.

IMPROVISATION AND FILM ACTING

Improvisation, especially in its simplest forms, is not unlike charade games played at Christmas. It is a way of involving group members in dramatic activity. Many theatrical groups use this approach for the development of characters on the stage but there is a world of difference, however, between a film and a stage performance. This is one of the main discoveries which each member of a group should make. Before any serious work can be undertaken it is essential that a film group be prepared to take part in a number of sessions of dramatic work, without the presence of a cine-camera.

The best way to begin, whether at home or in a large hall, is to sit all the members of the group in a circle. This circle then becomes a stage. Many different kinds of exercises develop once initial embarrassment has been overcome: give one member of a group a single word upon which to improvise; once the first member has begun, any other member may join in, as and when he sees fit. Any performance relies for its impact upon co-operation between members, and its success will be in direct proportion to the amount of effort and imagination which is put in. Those not involved in the improvisation automatically become the audience. Good imaginary settings for improvisations usually include: the bus-stop, the waiting-room, the railway carriage (coach). These are all chosen because they invite some kind of dramatic response even from the most timid members.

Group improvisation is important because it brings group members into closer contact with one another. They learn what it is like to stand up and look each other in the eye. A group must pass through the initial maze of blushes and giggles, otherwise they will never progress. A film group almost always has the same audience when shooting a film – each other. For this reason it is essential that they learn to work together, usually an enjoyable process.

The portrayal of character must be given serious consideration. Jean Paul Belmondo in *Breathless (A Bout de Souffle)*, 1959

The introduction of the cine-camera should be done with the minimum of ostentation, and the minimum of technical instruction. If the group is still working in a circle, the best thing is to put the camera on an empty chair. The whole group should be told which piece of the camera to look through and which piece of the camera makes it go. Provided there is enough light, that is all they need to know. Improvisation takes place as usual, but individual members are encouraged to pick up the camera and film parts of what is happening. The stress is put on catching the *relevant* parts of any action or performance. The actors are required to ignore the camera and continue with their work. One reel of 8 mm. film shot at each of these sessions is quite adequate and very cheap.

The first problem is to learn to relax. Then you must look critically at your own efforts. Each improvisation you do will help you to understand the importance of a slight change in expression, or the movement of an arm or leg. When the camera is used, try to look for these points in the performance of other group members, and record them on film. Never accept what you think is second rate. Try filming one gesture or expression in several different ways. Do not be frightened to hold the camera on one person for a long time. Practise subtle changes of expression in front of a mirror. This avoids the embarrassment of an audience while you are learning. Remember that concentration and involvement will bring success.

The following week, when the film has returned from the processing laboratories, it should be viewed just as it is, without any editing. The group will be quite happy to look at it two or three times. When the laughter has died down serious discussion can follow. What the group must look for is whether this piece of film has recorded information which has any meaning at all. Everyone will remember clearly the improvisations of the previous session. What needs to be established is whether these improvisations have worked successfully on film. There are two main aspects which must be examined closely: the first is the *way* in which the filming has been done; the second is in the performances of group members. These are closely related.

Up till now no mention has been made of camera work. The first filming will probably be in the style of a newsreel cameraman. Whatever lectures the group may have had on camera technique, the length of shots, speed of panning, etc., results are usually similar at this stage. The advantage of the former method of working is that members of the group are not *told* exactly what makes a piece of film successful. They *discover* what it is through experience and by the mistakes they may make. These mistakes are discussed on the most simple level. Perhaps the character one wishes to see may be out of frame completely. Recognition of such obvious points as this make for rapid progress. Members soon realize how important it is to control the movements of the camera while filming.

Then comes an assessment of performance. Generally everyone agrees that if no one knew what the improvisations were about it would be impossible to tell from the reel of film. To begin with, lack of sound and the lack of a plot are given as reasons for this confusion. Sooner or later, however, specific points will be made about performances: 'Fred looks too stiff', or 'Angela's face looks terrified' are the kind of comments which are made. From this stage you can progress to exercises that are essentially filmic in character. Before you can obtain the best performances from a film group the presence of the cine-camera must be acknowledged and then so fully accepted that its presence can be ignored. A session can profitably be spent where members are asked to look at the camera as though it were an object or a person. Each shot should be a close-up of ten or fifteen seconds' length. Such subjects for each shot could be: looking at the camera as though it were a person you either like or dislike; treating the camera lens as though it were a mirror (a girl could be putting on make-up as she looked at the camera lens); having something in one's eye.

The results of this kind of exercise are always interesting and they bring us to the stage where a close examination of the qualities of facial expression is possible. The camera can be quite static for each shot. Other exercises may be devised which involve movement of the body. Six different shots may be taken of people entering a room and sitting in a chair; they may be asked to look tired or happy or worried when they come in. Members can learn to gauge from personal experience what they have to do to achieve a desired effect. All this work is cheap and can be carried out over a period of a few weeks. It is from exercises such as this that you can progress to the type of film work mentioned in earlier chapters.

THE FACE IN FILM ACTING

There is probably no more expressive and revealing shot in film than a close-up of a face. A pair of eyes or a mouth and nose may be enlarged many times. Because of this enlargement the camera can show the slightest movement or change of expression. A pair of eyes moving from side to side can say more than the most violent action. It is essential that members of a group come to realize this. Because the camera is so sensitive to any nuance of expression you often need to *underplay* a sequence. This has been mentioned in relation to editing and is even more noticeable in acting. Often the necessary facial expression can be *implied* by its *placing* in relation to other shots. If a woman walks into a room and discovers the murdered body of her boyfriend on the floor, it is seldom necessary for her immediate reaction to be a violent contortion of all the muscles of the face. A cut from the discovery to a close-up of the woman's face will be enough. The

Improvisation exercises

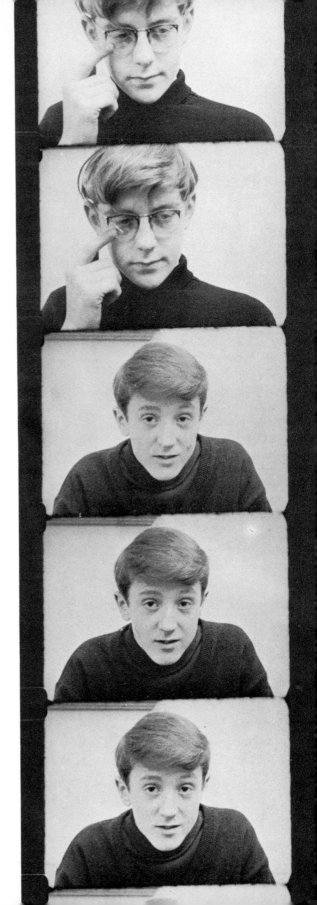

49

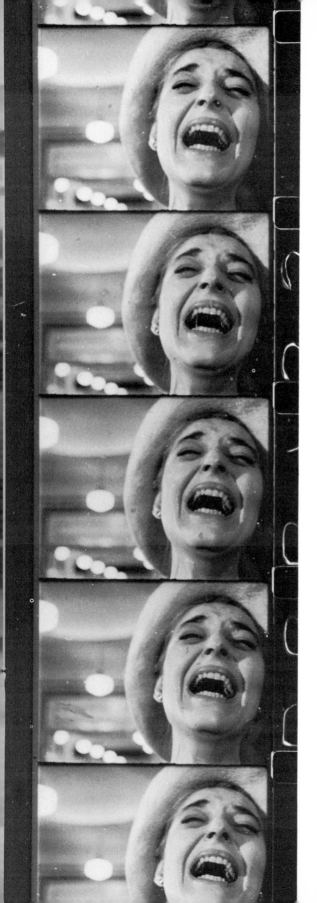

audience itself then goes through the awful realization of what has happened at the same time as the character concerned. In fact the woman may have been staring at a pile of cables on the floor when the particular close-up was taken. It is the *placing* of the shot in context which gives it its dramatic force.

A film group should devise its own exercises to explore these characteristics of facial expression. As time goes by it will become obvious that for any shot of the face to have a meaning it must be seen as an integral part of a film. There are times when very strong emotional feeling has to become the whole content of one particular shot. This requires either a wealth of acting experience or else total commitment on the part of the actor concerned. It can be seen opposite – these are not stage tears. It is better for a group to let editing aid the actors' performance until they are sure that strong emotion can be shown convincingly in a single shot. These are the factors which make short film exercises so important if a group is to make a serious statement on film.

These are not 'stage' tears. Anne Bancroft in *The Pumpkin Eater*, 1964

The way in which an actor walks, turns, runs, or moves his arms is also of importance. The paradox here is that the best performance is usually obtained when the actor is least conscious of his own body. This is why all film exercises should be designed to overcome self-consciousness. It is surprisingly difficult to look natural when you begin using film. A character in a film may be required to show visually that he has just remembered something of importance. In film, an actor may be tempted to make an exaggerated gesture such as clapping his hands to his face, then frowning deeply. In real life his reaction might well be to suck his teeth and stop what he was doing for a moment. How, for instance, does a man register surprise on entering a room? Where does his eye fall? Does it glance from an object to the right, then to the left, then rest on another completely motionless until eventually you see a flicker of emotion in his eyes; is he silent? Does he breathe heavily? Learn to observe emotion and expression of emotion in reality and you will soon realize how unnecessary overstatement is.

It may be that a film group wishes to experiment with a form of silent film-making. In this type of work a great deal of emphasis rests on the importance of cinematic mime. All movements and gestures take on a more stylized air. The work can be valuable and rewarding, as long as the group understands what it is trying to do.

The type of characters to be portrayed
At a school play we expect to see Julius Caesar or Macbeth played by a seventeen-year-old schoolboy. We are also used to the biggest and plumpest boy in the school playing the part of a policeman. A film group should avoid this kind of situation whenever possible. If a man of fifty is required for a film and there is no man of fifty in the group, I would suggest that either you find a man of fifty or make a different film. Disguising age is fraught with difficulties and demands an indulgent audience. It is far better for a group to accept its members as being a particular age or type. This limitation is quite acceptable. Through the work suggested in this chapter groups will discover the type of characters they can handle with conviction. They will even find that the most aggressive person looks meek on the screen and vice versa. It is this kind of problem which a group *can* examine and successfully overcome.

THE ACTOR AND THE DIRECTOR
Every member of a film group should gain some experience of directing. While film is essentially a group activity, it is the director who has the final say as to how a film is to be made. If any special performances are required from actors, it is the director who must elicit these performances.

There is a famous story about the director Alfred Hitchcock. He was once quoted as saying that all actors are cattle. When questioned about this by an interviewer, he said he had been misunderstood. 'Actors,' he said, 'are not cattle – they should be treated like cattle!'

This statement typifies just one approach to directing. Some directors do not like their actors to have too much idea of what is going on. They prefer to let them learn their lines, get on the set, and do nothing more or less than what they are told. It has even been suggested that the best film actors are people who cannot 'act' at all in the accepted sense of the word. They do, however, possess the ability to *relax completely* in front of a barrage of cameras.

At the other end of the scale there is the director who will speak to an actor for hours before he shoots any film. His concern is to explore all the many feelings the particular character is supposed to have and discuss these feelings with the actor. This director is particularly aware and sensitive to his actors so that he seems to possess the power of almost entering the mind of the actor; to be so attuned to him that he can communicate and elicit from his actors the exact nuance he requires.

The average film group will work in a somewhat more modest way. The director will achieve a healthy compromise in his approach. A good idea is for the whole group to sit round and discuss how each character is to be interpreted. Improvisation with a tape-recorder can be valuable in this context. From detailed discussion the director can decide how a particular part is to be played. He must be sure that the actors have overcome any problems of embarrassment before shooting starts as film groups can seldom afford to take any shot more than once. Discussion also avoids the director turning into a bully. Critical encouragement and consideration will obtain the best performances.

STAGE AND SCREEN ACTING

There are many differences between a screen performance and a stage performance. This will become slowly apparent to members of a film group. Some of the differences have been mentioned, but it is worth a little more examination. They are primarily concerned with the texture of reality in film. The only thing which can save a badly acted film is an outstanding plot or a superb display of imagery. Neither of these is readily available for a film group. The deficiencies in play-acting are often disguised under an eloquent soliloquy or biting wit supplied by the author. On stage an actor can give a blustering caricature performance which will carry the audience with it. This is not true of film.

The writer Dudley Nichols has clarified this important aspect of acting on the screen:

'Unthinking people speak of the motion picture as the medium of "action", the truth is that the stage is the medium of action while the screen is the medium of reaction. It is through identification with the person *acted upon* on the screen and not with the person acting, that the film builds up its oscillating power with an audience.'

The classic example of this, of course, is the gangster film where the hero is about to face terrible consequences if he does not tell the villains the whereabouts of the money. While the villains threaten, cajole or physically assault the hero, we spend more time watching him than them. We often see him in close-up and wonder with the villains whether he will crack under the strain.

This brings us back to the calibre of performance expected from a film actor. In the example just quoted it is the editing which will condition the audience's response to the film. If the hero sits motionless and expressionless throughout the scene, it is more likely to be successful than if he is constantly scowling and frowning. Those involved in group film-making should remember the importance of *underplaying* their part. By deliberately not acting a good screen performance is within the grasp of anyone, an important fact in a film group where, unlike the film industry, every member should be an actor.

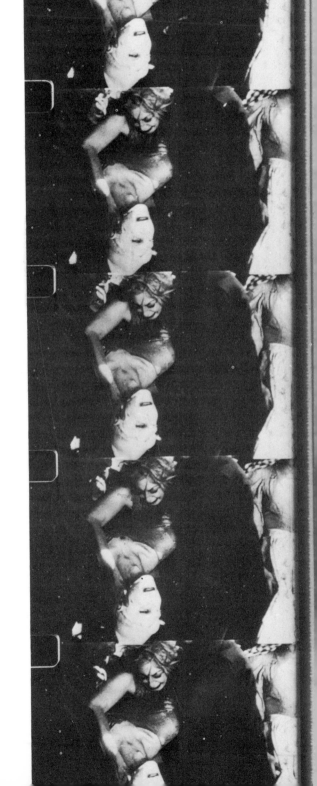

The more formal screen performance is reminiscent of the theatre. *Sawdust and Tinsel*, 1953

Sound

Most amateur film groups use sound to enhance their films. Suitable music is chosen which enriches mood and pace. This is quite acceptable but it does tend to deny sound its full power as an integral part of a film. It may be true that any sound is better than no sound but it is also true that *considered* sound is better still. The practical approaches to the use of sound will be examined in a moment. First we must examine the types of sound-track available to the average film group.

THE COMMENTARY

The straight commentary is the least complex way of adding a human element to a sound-track but in general it is unsuitable to a film which has dramatic content. This is because it is difficult to commentate on a specific dramatic situation without describing what is already on the screen. There is, however, a derivation from the straight commentary which can be extremely valuable. This has come to be known as the *voice-over* technique. Instead of hearing an unidentified voice, the audience hears the 'thoughts' of one or more of the characters on the screen.

We may see a sequence of film which shows a young man walking down the street. This in itself can mean many different things. The voice on the sound-track may run something like this: 'So they told me that I was unsuitable for the job and they were very sorry. Had to have better marks at English, at least, before they could possibly consider me. Now what? I suppose I'll go back to the employment agency next week and try again. Another stupid waste of time.' This simple example shows the power which the voice-over technique lends to a film and relieves the film-maker of tedious visual explanations. Without this short piece of sound we would have had to show a sequence something like this:

1 Young man outside a block of offices. He is holding an appointment card.
2 Sign in window reading 'Vacancies for qualified men'.
3 Man waiting for interview.
4 The interview and refusal.
5 Young man leaving the building.

As you can imagine, this last treatment is time-consuming and finally rather unconvincing. Yet it is quite possible from the first treatment to believe that all this has happened to the young man. His frame of mind and the problem of unemployment are quickly established. We are given more time to study him as a character.

WILD SOUND

This type of sound may be used to provide the general background to a film. For example, the noise of traffic in the street. It can also be the main content of a sound-track. A film may show an incident in a crowded fair-ground. The sound can then be that of people shouting, roundabouts, barrel-organs, etc. Very little speech is necessary.

EFFECTS

The wind in the trees or a door-bell ringing or a gunshot are the kind of sounds known as effects. The longer effects are practical for a film group, but a gunshot can lead to problems of synchronization. Groups should build up a gallery of effects on tape. Remember again that effects should add subtly to the overall scene.

MUSIC

This includes all forms of musical background from a single instrument to a full orchestra. It is probably the best way to induce a particular mood.

A word should be said here about problems of copyright. All radio broadcasts and commercial recordings on tape or record are rigidly protected by a Copyright Act. Strictly speaking you should not re-record any of these even in the privacy of your own home. This does not work in practice, but a film group has to be more careful. Unless the film is to be shown to a very limited audience of friends and family a group will open themselves to prosecution if they use commercial recordings. This is a very regrettable situation as some of the best sound material is automatically kept out of one's hands. There are certain records which may be bought specifically as sound effects but these offer little scope and the music tends to sound artificial. If you have a friend who plays the guitar or the violin, see if he will play for you. Certain types of music lend themselves to improvisation,

Without sound every statement is over-emphasized

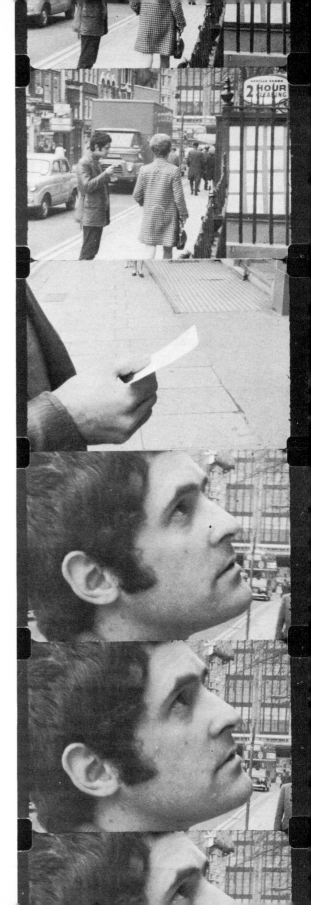

notably jazz and flamenco. If these are used the musicians can improvise as they watch the picture. They can react to changes of pace or moments of drama. With a few rehearsals this method produces good results. All solo instruments can lend quality to a sound-track if the musicians are in sympathy with the film. Decide on the general qualities you wish your music to have, then make a determined effort to find a local group or individual who can help you. The simplest music can be successful when carefully balanced with effects and voices. *The music must be chosen or composed in relation to the quality of the images and the dramatic content of the film.*

There are three basic approaches open to a film group considering the type of sound which they will use:

1 *The sound-to-picture approach*
Here the film has been fully edited before final consideration is given to the sound-track. It can be successful but be sure that it is more than a way of filming in an embarrassing silence. There is no reason why a film group should not make silent films as long as they are aware that these films have a medium of their own. The silent film had a beautiful and poetic language which embodied many characteristics of mime. As sound film developed characters and events had to be portrayed in a more restrained manner. The tendency for a film group is to create an unhealthy compromise which is tentatively held together with a piece of music. If the voice-over technique is to be used, however, a comparatively high degree of synchronization is possible. This makes the sound less arbitrary.

2 *The picture-to-sound approach*
In this case the final sound-track is prepared first and the film is shot around it. It is valuable for groups who need a rigid skeleton of the *content* of their film but wish to retain a degree of freedom in the manner of shooting. If a longer film is being shot on a minimum of film stock, this approach is ideal. It does have the limitation that the film is committed once the sound-track has been prepared.

3 *The synthetic approach*
This is a combination of the two previous approaches, involving a preparatory sound-track which is modified as the film progresses.

Whichever of these methods is used, serious consideration must be given to sound from the outset. It does not matter if the film is to be four minutes or one hour in length.

THE TAPE-RECORDER AND SCRIPTING

A tape-recorder is most useful when scripting. This is because many group members find it difficult to express ideas on paper. Working with a tape-recorder allows an idea to grow quite naturally. It also has the advantage that it involves several members at the same time and this ensures some diversity in approach which helps ideas to stay fresh.

The group begin by taking a chosen incident which is explained to each member. This incident is then improvised as recording. It is repeated several times and discussed. Members change parts and try to establish what is of importance in the characters and incidents. They discuss the kind of things the characters may say to each other or think. From this a treatment for the film is built up. The improvisation may also be done with music or wild sound in the background. Working in this way avoids unnecessary caricature. A tape-recorder allows all the obvious treatments and clichés to be done away with cheaply and enjoyably.

SYNCHRONIZATION

There are three degrees of synchronization, the first of which hardly qualifies for the term. It is the kind of sound intended to run continuously while the film is being projected and usually takes the form of music or wild sound such as the noises of a crowded station, etc. It is an *enhancing* sound-track.

The second method is concerned with synchronization to a fraction of a second. The sound and film are still run separately, the sound being on quarter-inch tape. There are on the market certain devices known as 'synchronizers'. These enable the projector and tape-recorder to run accurately together. If a synchronizer is not available, you still obtain good synchronization by having a 'start' mark on both tape and film.

The third method of synchronization is by far the most reliable and, not surprisingly, the most expensive. It involves the use of a magnetic stripe on the film. This stripe acts in exactly the same way as ordinary magnetic tape. It can be erased and a new sound-track be imposed at any time. The stripe can be put on the film at home or by laboratories and may be used on 8 mm., Super 8 or 16 mm. film. The projector which shows this type of film is a projector and tape-recorder in one. A microphone is provided with the projector for direct commentary or a fully prepared tape with mixed tracks may be transferred to the stripe on the film. Whether or not a group possesses this kind of equipment there are many common factors in the preparation of a sound-track and these will be examined in relation to specific examples.

The sound-to-picture approach

As already mentioned, this method requires that the film be fully edited with any necessary titles added before the sound-track is composed. The example here goes back to the simple four-minute film, though the same process applies irrespective of the film's length.

Example:

The film shows a girl sitting in a café. She is eating a plate of spaghetti. A boy is sitting opposite her. From time to time she looks at him. After a time a second boy walks in. His dress is unorthodox. The first boy gets up and leaves. The film ends with a shot of the girl looking at him. She then returns to eating her spaghetti.

As a silent film the audience may draw certain conclusions from what they see. The sound will clarify the film-maker's intentions. In order to explain how the sound was recorded here is a description of the layout of the recording room. There is a cupboard at the back which has a hole sawn in the door. This is filled with a sheet of thick plate glass. There is a tape-recorder and a record-player in the room. The boy and the girl are seated in front of the screen with a microphone placed between them. The record-player is on the other side of the room. The walls and ceiling of the room are lined with egg-boxes (collected by members of the group). These boxes act as acoustic tiles.

The first thing which is done is to put a pin scratch on *one frame* at the beginning of the film, before the titles. Each time the film is projected this scratch will show as a clear flash of light on the screen.

The tape-recorder is set to *record* and started. A member of the group speaks into the microphone: 'Sound-track – Café Story'. He then claps his hands in front of the microphone. The tape is rewound and played back. It is stopped when the clap is exactly over the play-back head. The machine is set to record. The record-player with the required music is turned on and a level is set to record directly through the microphone. The boy and the girl then speak into the microphone so that the level for their voices may be set. The projector is set up in the cupboard. It has already been focused and the flash frame is well down on the film leader. This avoids several false starts because members do not see the flash.

When this simple procedure has been carried out, the first recording may be made. The projector is started *first*. The moment the flash frame appears on the screen the tape-recorder is started. In the case of the example, quoted the sound-track was improvised. It ran something like this:

Sound	Picture
Music fades in, then down, and continues in background.	Girl eating spaghetti.
1ST BOY: She's nice. I'd like to know her. Nice hair. I think I'll go and speak to her.	Boy sitting-looking Girl eating. Boy looking.
GIRL: Why does he keep on looking at me when I'm eating my spaghetti? It's enough to put anyone off. I wish I could see exactly what he looks like.	Girl eating. Looking over at boy.
1ST BOY: Why am I always so scared to go up and speak to girls? This one looks different. I really will go over and speak to her. I will.	Boy looking. Girl glances at boy.
GIRL: He's not so bad looking really. I wonder if he is going to speak to me. I hope he does. He's really quite nice.	Cuts back and forth from boy to girl.
1ST BOY: God – What's this? Why is he sitting so near her? I always have my chances ruined by someone like this. If he touches her I'll hit him.	Cut to café door. 2nd boy enters, sits near girl. Examines her closely from top to bottom. Cut to girl looking at 2nd boy.
GIRL: I feel as though he is undressing me with his eyes.	

1ST BOY: Ah well! I bet she finds him more attractive than me. Perhaps it's just as well. I don't really care.

Cut to 1st boy looking at other two.

GIRL: Oh don't tell me he's going. Just when I thought he would come over to speak to me. What a pity. He did look quite nice.

1st boy gets up to leave.

He smiles sheepishly at door.

Music fades up then down.

GIRL: Oh well! Just one of those days. Food . . . that's the only thing left for me.

Cut to girl. Watches him go. Her face expressionless. She returns to her spaghetti.

Music up then slowly out.

End

The film and tape are marked for synchronization

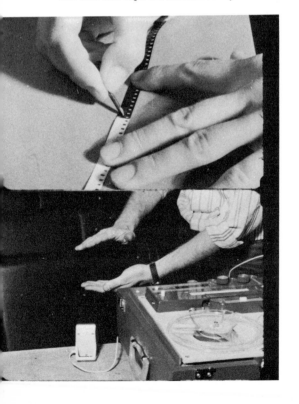

When this recording is finished, both tape and film are rewound. The clap is once again placed over the replay head of the tape-recorder, but this time the controls are set to *replay*. The projector is started in the same manner as before. The instant the flash appears on the screen the tape is started. This time it is possible to view what may be the finished film. It is quite simple to prepare several sound-tracks for any one film. Often a member has an unsuitable voice for the part which he or she may have played in this film and this can be substituted for another on the sound-track. Experiment with dubbing characters' voices and you will discover that this is yet another way of exploring the many possible interpretations of a simple piece of film.

You should experiment with one film. See what happens if three different sound-tracks are recorded. In the first the voices should be soft and friendly. The second should have a more aggressive dialogue and the third make use of lengthy pauses in sound while you watch the action taking place. This experiment can be repeated with romantic music on the first track, martial or dramatic music on the second, and wild sound on the third.

If your film has been shot in a railway station, go out and record the sounds of porters, shooting trains entering and leaving the station. Play this sound in the background when recording your final sound-track and notice the difference it makes.

The marked film projected through a door

The picture-to-sound approach

This is inevitably a more rigid way of working and means the use of a stop-watch. The sound must be prepared accurately and definitively before any film is shot. We will assume that you have made the film just quoted by using this method. The improvised dialogue and simple mixing of sound would have been done *first*. Each specific section would then have been timed, and a shooting script prepared around these timings. Each shot has to allow a small overlap of time, e.g. a shot of the girl eating spaghetti which is due to last ten seconds would be taken for twelve seconds in the camera.

The editing of the picture is now somewhat more complex. It must be done on the editing bench. Tables are available which show the exact number of frames per second when any gauge of film is projected. Working on 8 mm. this sometimes means counting the frames by hand. Once this has been done the shots may be assembled clearly and logically. The method of synchronization for this and the previous approach are identical, i.e. the tape and film are marked in the same manner.

If the group is fortunate enough to possess a magnetic projector, this method is a good way of working. Once the film has been shot and edited, the sound-track is transferred on to the magnetic stripe on the film and will always remain in synchronization.

The synthetic approach

As a group gains experience in the use of film with sound it inevitably becomes more ambitious. When a film is more complex it is often found that a combination of the two previous approaches is the answer. In this way a complicated sound-track may be built up which needs very little equipment for its preparation. Naturally, a sound-mixer and three tape-recorders will produce finer quality sound, but groups should not feel deterred if they only possess one tape-recorder.

It should be mentioned that for simple synchronization when the tape-recorder and projector are not linked in any way it is advisable to use the *same* two pieces of equipment. This will help to ensure that variation in the speed of different machines will not destroy the synchronization.

Whichever method is used your sound-tracks should always be conceived as an integral part of the film.

Lighting

A group may make several films without any artificial lighting. But there are times when the use of lights is unavoidable. Once the situation arises the group must decide whether it is trying to emulate the professionals. In terms of the group-made film this can mean that one member of the group becomes a lighting fanatic. He will insist that several lights are essential when one would be adequate. The purpose of this chapter is to suggest some approaches to lighting which will enable all group members to light a scene simply and successfully. (In this way all jobs are interchangeable.) Lighting is as much a creative activity as shooting and editing. It should be constantly open to experiment and discovery, never a dull pedantic affair. There are many helpful books giving general or specific information on what to do with lights but there is no doubt that the best way for a group to learn about lighting is by *doing it*.

TYPES OF LIGHTING EQUIPMENT

Photofloods

The simplest form of lighting equipment is the photoflood lamp. These lamps and their reflectors are cheap and lightweight (page 63). Clamps may be purchased which fit on the back of the reflector and enable the light to be hand-held or attached to a post or ledge. The main disadvantage with the cheapest photoflood lamps is that they have a very short life. They are overrun heavily when lit and will burn for no more than about three hours when switched on continuously. Some of the more expensive photofloods have a longer life. Any photographic dealer can advise as to specific cost and running life. They are the ideal light for titling or any photo-copying work. Occasionally one may use photofloods without reflectors in order to produce a more diffuse light. They may also be purchased with inbuilt reflectors which give a highly directional light.

A more expensive floodlight is also shown on page 63. This light has a large white reflector with a diameter of about 3 feet.

Quartz lamps

Quartz lamps have caused a revolutionary change in lighting for amateurs and professionals and have a great many advantages. They are small, lightweight, silent, and extremely powerful. A gas is sealed in the lamp. This gas reduces blackening on the bulb. A 1000-watt quartz bulb is about 5 inches long and a quarter of an inch in diameter (page 64). They are available either as lights which are designed to be hand-held or in a more sturdy form for studio work. Most of these lamps can have clamps attached to them making them extremely portable. They are available as floodlights or spots.

They have one disadvantage; they become extremely hot if left on for more than a few minutes. If placed in the corner of a room without due care, they will scorch wallpaper and blister paint; all parts of the light except the handle or stand become so hot that they will burn anyone who touches them. This is not to suggest that they are dangerous – rather that they should be handled with care.

They are initially more expensive, costing at least four times as much as a simple photoflood. Their burning time does increase considerably.

EXPOSURE ON CINE-FILM

Whether you are filming in black and white or colour the exposure of the film must be correct. This means that when the film is running through the camera each frame of film is exposed to exactly the required amount of light for that particular film stock.

Good exposure is determined by two things – the speed of the shutter and the size of the aperture.

SHUTTER SPEED

When a film is run through a cine-camera the shutter speed remains constant. This means that given a particular shutter speed, the adjustment of the aperture is all-important.

APERTURE

Marked on the lens mount of nearly every camera may be found some or all of the following set of figures:

1.4 2 2.8 4 5.6 8 11 16 22

There will be a pointer or a mark on the lens to which any of these figures may be aligned. Each one of these figures represents a change in aperture or *stop*. There is an adjustable diaphragm within the lens mount which enables this to be done.

Moving from one *f*-number to another either *doubles* or *halves* the size

Photofloods

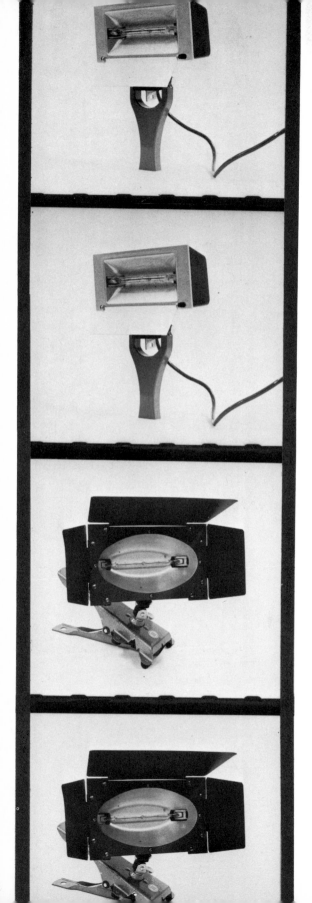

of the aperture. Hence it doubles or halves the *exposure*.

The smaller the f-number the larger the aperture.

Exposure should always be accurate to within *half a stop*. The best way to gauge a particular exposure is by the use of a photoelectric exposure meter.

PHOTOELECTRIC EXPOSURE METERS

An example of a good photoelectric exposure meter is shown on page 66. The principles on which this type of meter works are simple. The light which enters the meter falls upon a photoelectric cell. When light reaches this cell it generates a minute electric current. This current moves the pointer of an extremely sensitive microammeter. The pointer or needle moves across a specially calibrated set of scales. (In the light meter, page 66, from 0–16.) The number against which the pointer stops is noted. The rotating discs on meter enable one to read quickly and easily the required aperture for a particular shutter speed.

The main point to remember is that there is always some kind of needle which passes over a calibrated scale. Used with care a photoelectric meter should be very accurate (to within one-third of a stop).

When a reading has been taken, the required aperture must be set on the lens. Some cameras have their light meters built in. If this is the case, the adjustment to the camera is done by means of a camera stop control (in a semi-automatic camera) or if fully automatic the meter sets the stop automatically.

There are two basic types of light meters: *incident* and *reflected*. Some meters such as the one illustrated are convertible.

A reflected light meter measures the amount of light reflected from the subject. An incident light meter measures the light falling upon a subject.

Quartz lamps

REFLECTED LIGHT METERS

This type of light meter is pointed from the camera towards the subject. Whenever possible take the meter close to the subject. If you can point the meter slightly downwards when filming out of doors; the meter's angle of vision is often wide enough to take too much account of the light of the sky and this leads to under-exposure. The following points may be helpful:

1   If the contrast between subject and background is not too great, the meter reading can be taken as correct.
2   If the contrast is harsh between subject and background, two readings should be taken – one of the subject and one of the background. The exposure given should be half-way between the two readings. There may, however, be times when you wish to expose only for the subject at the risk of over- or under-exposing the background.

All meters built in to cameras work on the reflected light principle.

INCIDENT LIGHT METERS

Readings with this type of meter are taken from the position of the subject. Two readings are normally taken – one with the meter pointed at the camera, the other with the meter pointed towards the light source. The exposure should be half-way between these two readings. The white cone page 66 shows how the meter can be converted for incident light readings. It is the cone which is pointed at both the camera and light source.

One distinct advantage of an incident light meter is that it can provide an accurate guide for the exposure of face tones.

Ideally, you should possess your own meter and never use any other. Experience is the best aid to taking a light reading.

THE USE OF LIGHTS

For the average film group the rule should be never to use lights unless absolutely necessary.

Tungsten lighting should *never* be mixed with daylight when shooting colour film. Tungsten light, however powerful it may appear, contains a strong element of red. Daylight contains a strong element of blue. Colour film has to be specially balanced for use with artificial or daylight. If a daylight film is used in artificial light it will appear very pink where the tungsten light has been strongest. An artificial light film used in daylight appears correspondingly blue.

Filters are available to convert one type of film to another. Some manufacturers produce only one type of colour film for Super 8 cameras. The camera then has a built-in filter which can be clicked into position for the chosen type of light.

None of these problems occur when using black-and-white film. It is then quite permissible to supplement daylight with artificial light.

When filming in a room the light is always directional. This means that a figure near the window will appear well-lighted from one side while the other will be in heavy shadow. There are two ways of overcoming this problem:

(a) The use of reflectors

A white sheet or board or a mirror may be used as a reflective surface. A reflector is especially useful for close-up shots. It will throw light into the shadow side of a subject and help to reduce the contrast ratio. A reflector may be used with artificial light or daylight.

(b) The use of tungsten light

Tungsten light gives the cameraman control over the direction and intensity of light. A strong light can take the place of a window. For simple film work two photofloods are adequate. One of these becomes the main or *key* light. The other takes the place of a reflector and is used to lighten areas of shadow. For normal lighting the two lamps would be placed at right-angles to the subject and the camera would be placed somewhere within the right-angle. Occasionally more than two lights may be necessary for some special effect such as back or top lighting.

Quartz lamps are ideal for normal filming. One lamp can give enough

Light meters

light to fill an average-size room. Because they are so powerful, these lights are seldom pointed straight at the subject, but are reflected off walls or ceiling. With a little experience it is possible to achieve many interesting effects using only one quartz lamp which has been hand-held.

Special effects

Most rules are made to be broken. Some of the most interesting lighting effects are obtained in this way. Shooting straight into the lights at night while people are passing to and fro can produce worth-while images. The possibilities for experiments with lighting effects are endless: close-up lighting, silhouette effects, distant or misty lighting effects. There are also times when a more 'academic' form of lighting is required. The important thing is that a group should experiment with methods of lighting and always seek the most satisfying solution to each particular problem of distribution or changing quality.

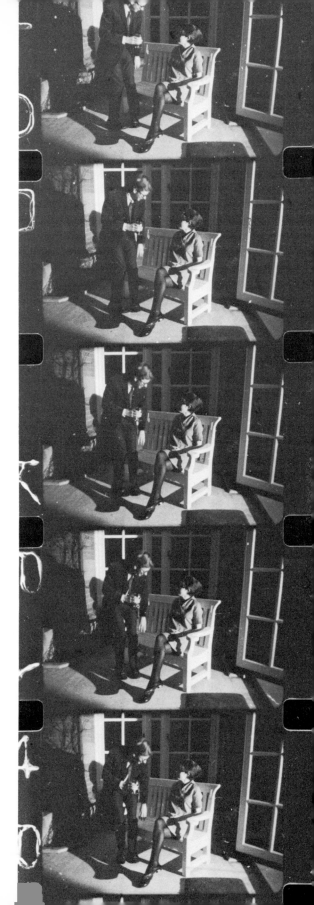

A scene which required only one quartz lamp to light it

LIGHTING FOR MOVEMENT

When lighting for still photography the lights have to be correct from one position for a fraction of a second only. Lighting for cine-film has to take into account the fact that figures will be moving within a given area. This is why the use of general lighting is advisable in early stages of work. Before he starts shooting the cameraman should always make sure that the person he is filming has enough light on him wherever he may be standing or sitting.

LIGHTING AND DEPTH OF FIELD

Depth of field means the distance either side of a subject in which near and far objects are in satisfactory focus. Some cameras have fixed focus lenses. They will then be in focus from about eight feet to infinity. Provided the subject is at least eight feet from the camera there will be no problems.

More expensive cameras have variable focusing facilities. This enables the cameraman to deliberately choose which part of the field he will have in focus. This will be discussed in more detail in relation to lenses. As far as lighting is concerned there are two important points to remember:

1 The stronger the intensity of light, the smaller the aperture of lens and vice versa.
2 The smaller the aperture of the lens, the greater the depth of field and vice versa.

A NOTE ON CABLES AND PLUGS

It is very important to have an adequate supply of extension cables for lighting. It is equally important that adaptors are made up to cover all possible types of sockets and conversions. This is a relatively inexpensive job and saves much time and trouble.

The points made here about lighting equipment are deliberately generalized in the hope that those with no previous knowledge can see the type of equipment that is available. The specific instructions for use of any piece of equipment are best obtained from the instruction manual. The exact number of burning hours of a lamp or its weight and dimensions are best obtained from a local photographic dealer. The important thing is to know what *kind* of information or piece of lighting equipment one needs.

EXERCISES INVOLVING LIGHTING TECHNIQUES

Opposite is example of lighting from a professional feature film. The composition within the frame is carefully balanced in areas of light and dark. The face in the mirror becomes the focal point, although it is surrounded by three areas of greater light intensity. The lighting cameraman has used a technique of strong chiaroscuro reminiscent of the late Renaissance painters in Italy. At the same time the image is never static in the film. The slightest movement of the woman's eyes becomes all important. This lighting, with its highly controlled arrangement of tones and shapes is not easily accessible to the average film group, especially from the purely practical point of

Professional lighting. *The Pumpkin Eater*, 1964

view such as lack of lighting equipment. We must, therefore, consider the type of effects which are possible with the minimum of lighting equipment. In lighting, as in other aspects of film-making, certain restrictions present a challenge which can prove to be an advantage.

Lighting cameraman, Walter Lassally, remarked on this in relation to his shooting of *The Loneliness of the Long Distance Runner*: ' . . . we shot the scenes in the Borstal in a tiny prefab up in north London, with no walls removed or anything like that. There were about twenty of us, actors and unit all jammed in there. It's quite a job, but it works and it gives an atmosphere. Up to a point such limitations are healthy because they force you away from the familiar pattern of lighting which arises from having it everywhere you want it. If you've got the whole set ringed with lamps and you can move them infinitesimally right or left, then you can do whatever you want. But this also leads to a kind of slackness, so that you don't, in fact, light it like real life. Limitations act as a good discipline. You are stimulated to work in a different way and you get a different look to the picture.'

Page 67 shows an example of a group film exercise which contained a night scene in the open air. The only light came through the French windows of the house. The normal light in the rooms was hardly enough to get a reading on a light meter and photofloods gave too dim a light source. They were also too directional. The answer was found by using a 1000-watt quartz lamp which was hand-held. It was not shone directly on to the couple but reflected off a wall. In this way the light was diffused and its intensity slightly lessened. While one would not want to make extraordinary claims for the image it provided, it was at least satisfactory.

Experiment with lighting exercises as part of the group's work. Devise exercises which rely on lighting for their effect: filming at a dance, for example.

Shooting directly into an artificial light source can help to create atmosphere or heightened atmosphere and lend added conviction to reality. Use colour and black-and-white film to explore these possibilities. Try exercises where the background is dark and only the figures are illuminated. See the strange quality faces take on if all the lighting is placed below eye-level. Deliberately place all lighting on one side of the subject and note the effect on tones and colours. Use exercises which concentrate on the placing of shadows for dramatic effect.

For members who wish to adopt a more logical approach, exercises should be purely observational. A reel of film may be taken of a single face. First one light, then two, may be placed in various positions with regard to height and distance from the subject. Each shot should be numbered and a diagram made of the placing of the lights. The aperture on the lens should also be noted. This type of work allows you to gauge accurately just what will happen in a given lighting situation. Ideally a group should try to balance 'scientific' lighting exercises against freer experimental work.

The texture of reality

This book has stressed simplicity of approach in film-making. The reasons for this will be explained more fully in this chapter and suggestions will also be made on the approach to a longer film. As time goes by, a film group must decide just what are its aims and policies. This is not as idealistic as it sounds. The mere factor of a group of people coming together and working is enough to justify its existence. But if the group is prepared to take film-making more seriously – a creative film-maker might say more *honestly*, then, perhaps to its surprise, even the most modest group will produce interesting and stimulating work. If you are an *honest* film-maker, your attitude to the interpretation of reality is of prime importance.

Take, for instance, this example: a group spends a great deal of time setting up one shot in a film and much trouble is taken to ensure that lighting and camera positioning are exact. The scene is one which shows a boy who is angry because he has to stay in and do his homework. Everyone in the group is concentrating so hard on technical problems that no one, not even the director, notices the boy's performance. The boy knows that he must show anger; that is all. The result is a series of shots which show a scowling face, clenched fists, stamping and kicking feet, cut against a shot of his friends playing outside. Yet, this sincere effort results in a thin replica of reality. Members of a film group should come to realize what is a convincing interpretation of reality.

Reality is a difficult and sometimes ambiguous term in relation to film. In this context it means that what is on the screen is seen by an audience who have completely suspended any sense of disbelief. For a film to be *real* it is not necessary for an audience to believe afterwards everything they have seen before the lights are turned on. The important thing is that *while* they are watching there must be no question of disbelief. Even if the film is a fantasy, the audience should feel that they have entered completely into this fantasy world; even to the extent of one member saying to another: 'Don't worry dear, it's only a film.'

THE PLOT AND THE PORTRAYAL OF REALITY

There is hardly any story that can be told that does not sound like another one which is already known. Because of this it is the *way* in which a story is told which becomes very important. We can no longer rely on an excellent plot to disguise poor film-making. The opposite is often the case. The importance of a good story to a film came about because film tried to follow in the steps of accepted literary tradition. Many novelists today are themselves rejecting the plot and looking for some other basis for their work. In terms of film it has meant that the director's emphasis is put on the relationship between characters, their environment, and portrayal.

SOCIAL ENVIRONMENT AND THE PORTRAYAL OF REALITY

Where the members of a film group live can be a constant source of inspiration for film material. Short films can be made which are designed to reflect the quality of local streets and places of amusement. Against this background may be set a simple incident involving members of the group. There is then no problem of finding a location for a particular film. The problem is which location to use. Instead of inventing a story and trying to decide where it might happen, take a location and ask 'What might happen here?' From this work a group can build up a fund of film material which can explore and establish the qualities of reality as portrayed on film. Until this has been done it is almost impossible to handle a story film with conviction.

Re-examine what is familiar and discover the dramatic and filmic possibilities in the seemingly ordinary. When you discover the potentialities of what can happen in a bus queue or at a café table you are sure to produce interesting film material. Whether a film is a high adventure or a simple incident taken from day to day living, it becomes real to an audience by the way in which it is presented. Familiarity blinds us to the properties of many things which we see, human or otherwise. This is why a camera has to *represent* reality in a new form. The stirring of a cup of tea or the putting on of a hat can become important by the startling quality of their 'ordinariness'.

People reflect the quality of their environment

73

Look for the qualities which typify for you the atmosphere of a place. Is it the people or the buildings or both? Try to record on film what distinguishes one person from another. Is it the way they walk, their clothes, or, perhaps, their age? Use a reel of film to record people who look happy or people who look bored; this will develop your confidence and help you to capture the transient aspects of reality.

THE DOCUMENTARY APPROACH

This is closely related to the group's own environment. It is excellent experience to produce several short documentary films on the type of locality where the group works and the people to be found there. Documentary has many advantages. For one thing, it provides a discipline as soon as a specific subject has been chosen. The subject can be clarified before any film is shot and research work can involve all members of the group.

An example of this type of work is a short film which shows the qualities of the main shopping centres in a particular area. The film can be shot so that there is a minimum of wastage or editing. Members should look for different types of shops and note the people who use them. They should try to illustrate visually the distinctive difference between an expensive private tailors' and a large department store, or the kind of food sold in a supermarket or a small delicatessen. It is a clear logical process. The visual comparison involves careful selection and this is an occupation in itself. The creativity evolves as a by-product of the main idea. This overcomes the time which is often wasted by needless soul-searching on the part of group members. No artist ever created anything by sitting down and thinking about his creative talents. It is only by actually *working* that something can be produced. The sound-track to a film such as this can be composed of comments by people who were out shopping. This visual and verbal comparison of ideas on a simple theme can be very effective and need not rely on too high a degree of sound synchronization.

Another approach is to compare through a film people of different age-groups. Set out with a cine-camera to see what old people do during the day. Try the magazine rooms in the library, park benches, and queues for early shows, these are the sort of locations where you may obtain the required information. The sound-track could be composed of comments by old people on the things that they do and what they think about.

Finally, a group may decide to make a short film about one particular person in their locality. This may be of interest because of his work or a hobby he pursues. He may even be of interest because he is such a very ordinary person. The sound-track for this kind of film could well be related in the first person.

Any of these documentary approaches are useful to a group in that they build a fund of visual information as well as providing experience of working with many different people. From a documentary can come an idea for a freer film which uses group members as its characters. It can be used as a form of reference notebook for any film group, as well as being a valid method of filming in its own right.

NEWSREEL TECHNIQUES OF FILMING

There is obviously a similarity between certain kinds of documentary approaches and news-reel filming. In both of these approaches the cameraman may have little or no idea of what will happen next. Some group members complain that with these techniques you cannot make a personal statement on film. This is certainly not the case: only in news-reel filming does the cameraman become the all-important figure. Moreover, it is through just this type of work that a cameraman can show what *he* considers is essential in what he sees. There is no script to work from. The techniques involved here are related to the filming of incidents mentioned earlier on page 73. If the cameraman is fully aware of what he sees and knows how to select the relevant points, he can become his own director. In the small group-made film this is often a more satisfactory situation.

THE DIFFERENT QUALITIES OF THE CINEMATIC IMAGE

There are always several ways to shoot any subject and it is vitally important for a group to become aware of this. A still photographer soon realizes that there are countless ways of composing a single picture, the cine-photographer, however, does not have the advantage of being able to alter the way a picture is framed in the enlarger. Once a piece of cine-film has been shot, that is how it must remain as far as composition goes. A camera which is following a figure has a constantly changing background, so that it would take months to work out whether the composition within the frame at any given time will be satisfactory.

The cinematic image often composes itself

Those who try to do this, unless they are very experienced, usually find that their film is unbearably formal and rigid, although it may contain moving images. There are some commercial film-makers who have managed to come to terms with this problem, notably the Italian director Michelangelo Antonioni. Because of the beauty of his cinematic compositions, he has been accused of 'artiness'. This kind of artiness is usually associated with a single figure shot against sunlight or two figures walking in front of a massive white concrete building, preferably in cinemascope. A shot like this included in a picture for its own sake *may* be termed as 'arty'.

Antonioni's own reply to this accusation is of great importance to the most humble film group. He states that *the beauty of a shot depends on whether or not it explains what it seeks to explain.* This should be the uppermost thought in the mind of any cine-cameraman. No training other than experience is necessary for a film group to be able to discover this truth. It is so simple that many young film enthusiasts find it difficult to understand. It demands of us that we do not spend all our time looking for the 'perfect shot', but that we concentrate on what we are trying to say through using film. If our motivation for filming is strong enough, the images will take care of themselves.

It is true that there are certain formal rules of composition in film. These rules are closely allied to types of pictorial composition in painting. Film composition like film language is something to be *discovered* rather than taught. For a film image to possess imposing or beautiful qualities it need not be carefully composed. This can be seen in the work of film-makers such as Richard Leacock. His films are seldom scripted and the images he obtains are a mixture of intuitive shooting and sheer practical necessity: composing a shot in the middle of a large crowd of people, for instance, is often impossible. The overall effect of this way of filming may be much more satisfactory than shots which are examined individually and the whole approach closer to the type of work a group is likely to produce in its initial stages.

APPROACHING THE LONGER FILM

When a group feel that they have come to a clear understanding of their own limitations and potentialities they will move inevitably towards the idea of making a longer film. A ten-minute film is probably the next step to be taken. One of the biggest problems with the longer film is that it is so complex to handle. Unlike the short film, the longer film requires a strong skeletal structure if it is to succeed. The long film will have a given number of important points which have to be put over. If it is a documentary, these points may be factual but in other kinds of film they may be purely dramatic. Whether or not a film has a strong story line, these essential points must be given just the right emphasis within the integral framework of the film. Constant discussion during editing is essential; second opinion is almost always of value as the editor can become oblivious to the simplest points through constantly viewing the same piece of film. It must also be mentioned that editing on the bench plays a more important part in the longer film. The method of working suggested earlier in the book is designed to prepare a group for the time when they tackle more complex problems. Until the shorter film can be successfully carried out from conception to completion, it is unwise to attempt any more ambitious projects.

A conservative attitude to film-making can be inhibiting and dampen enthusiasm; and once the basic principles of film-making have been grasped group members should be encouraged to take an interest in developments in the contemporary cinema. Although there is a danger that a superficial grasp of certain trends could lead to meaningless obscurity in a group's work, if these are examined with an open and intelligent mind they may provoke enthusiasm and lead a group to experiment and explore on its own. New ideas and techniques should be experimented with until they are properly mastered and understood. Then they can be incorporated into actual film-making rather than mere experiments.

Always master a technique before you include it in a film, and be careful to distinguish between an experiment and a finished product.

STREAM OF CONSCIOUSNESS IN FILM

The simplest type of film often shows the thoughts of a particular character in visual terms. As mentioned earlier, the thoughts of a character can be learnt by using the voice-over technique. The advantage of using a visual approach is that material from many different sources can be cut into one sequence. This portrayal of a series of events has been the concern of contemporary film-makers such as Joseph Strick, director of *Ulysses*. Because it is relatively simple as a technique, some group members may wish to try it. The playwright, Harold Pinter, has commented on this approach to film and what he has to say is of value to any film group:

'You see, suppose a character is walking down a lane, this lane, as we are. You could easily write down a stream of thought which might be perfectly accurate and believable, and then translate it into a series of images: road, field, hedge, grass, corn, wheat, ear, her ear on the pillow, tumbled hair, love, love years ago . . . But when one's mind wanders and associates things in this way it's perfectly unself-conscious. Do exactly the same thing in film and the result is precious, self-conscious, over-elaborate – you're using absurdly complex means to convey something very simple. Instead you should be able to convey the same sort of apprehension not by opening out, proliferating, but by closing in, looking close and closer, harder and harder at the things that are there before you.'

77

The story of a film

The general approach to film-making described in this book is equally applicable to the semi-professional film group. It is the purpose of this chapter to describe the kind of equipment which such a film group may use and the way in which a particular film was shot and edited. A general mystique has grown up in the film industry about the way a film is shot and put together. It is often very difficult to find out how sound does get on to film or the way in which sound and picture are kept in synchronization. The explanations offered here are very simple and are designed to provide the enthusiast with an overall picture of what happens when a film is made. The method of working described requires a small team (two or three people) for the scripting, shooting, and editing of a complete film.

THE CAMERA

Most semi-professional film groups use 16 mm. film. It is much cheaper than 35 mm. but can produce excellent results. Until recently almost all film shot for television was on 16 mm. Newsreel cameramen still use this gauge. The camera used for this type of work is usually battery operated. 16 mm. film is used by amateur film groups in 100-feet rolls. These last approximately two and a quarter minutes. The professional camera opposite has a 400-foot magazine on top. This enables the cameraman to shoot film for longer periods without stopping. It is easily portable when attached to a shoulder harness as in the illustration. The pistol grip allows the left hand to be kept free for operating the other controls such as focusing. When working outside the cameraman becomes a mobile tripod.

THE TAPE-RECORDER

A good tape-recorder is the second basic essential. Apart from recording sound of the highest quality, this recorder has another important feature. It will record *synchronous* sound. Synchronous sound means that the sound which accompanied each frame of film can be reproduced simultaneously when that frame of film is projected in other words one can have people talking on the screen.

SYNCHRONOUS SOUND

In order to produce synchronous sound, the camera and tape-recorder are linked by a cable. When sound and film are recorded a pulse runs along this cable from the camera into the tape-recorder. This marks the tape and ensures that perfect synchronization is obtained. The pulse may be thought of as a heart-beat which is fed along a life-line between camera and tape-recorder. When this pulse is received it registers on a dial on the recorder. It is known as a sync. pulse (synchronizing pulse). This enables the sound-recordist to keep a constant check that the pulse is being received. Without the pulse synchronization would be impossible.

THE EDITOR

The editing machine must be capable of reproducing both sound and picture. Page 80 shows one such machine. It will be seen that there are four spools on the machine for carrying film. The top two carry the picture which can be viewed as the film is run through. The bottom two carry the sound. This sound is on 16 mm. magnetic film. The sound is transferred from quarter-inch tape to magnetic film before editing commences. In any professional film, the sound and picture are separate for most of the time.

THE PICTURE SYNCHRONIZER

A professional film always has several sound-tracks. These separate tracks are synchronized on a picture synchronizer such as the one illustrated on page 80. This machine has a small viewer and up to three separate sound heads. These are all locked together. As the handle is turned the picture moves and the sound is heard through the small speaker which can be seen in the illustration. Each track has a separate volume control knob. In this way the tracks may be heard one at a time or all together. The machine also has an accurate footage counter which can be seen above the volume control knobs.

The pieces of equipment described here are typical of the sort used by all professional film units. The next section is a breakdown of the order in which things are done. Some smaller film units manage to by-pass some of these processes.

SCRIPTING

In the commercial film world the script is usually the means to obtaining financial backing. In the past a script or screenplay has been a very thorough document designed to show that the film-makers and scriptwriters are competent. This is still true of the bulk of expensive feature films. This degree of

The professional camera and tape-recorder

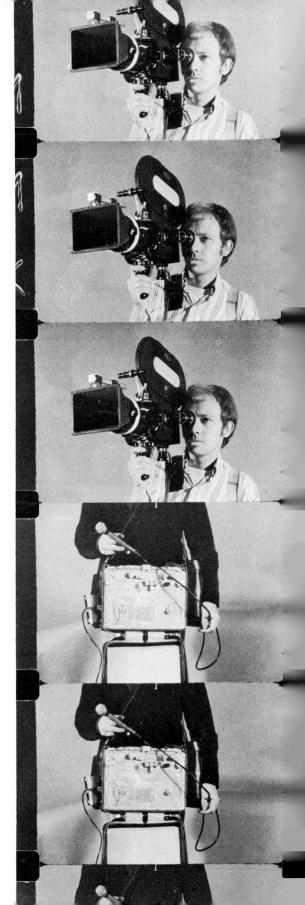

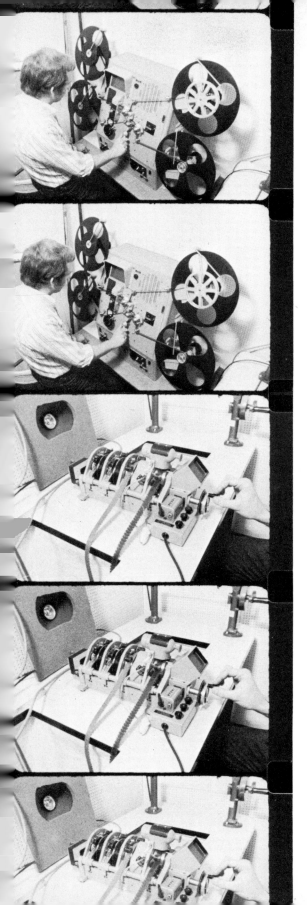

finalization at the scripting stage is not always necessary in a small production. Many fine documentaries have begun as a few scribbled notes on a sheet of foolscap. The type of film to be described here is one with a minimum amount of scripting. This film was shot spontaneously, with the cameraman selecting what he thought of relevance at the time of shooting.

BUDGETING

In this type of film the budgeting becomes more important than the actual script. A number of locations are chosen and a given footage of film allocated for each shooting session. The cameraman knows that he has a specified amount of film with which to work. In a commercial film the cost of film stock is a minor expense, but in a small semi-professional production it is very important. The following list suggests items to be included in the budget:

1 Film stock
2 Processing
3 Negative cutting
4 Opticals
5 Dubbing session
6 Magnetic film stock
7 White and black film spacer
8 Lighting spares
9 Transport
10 Editing and general extras such as chinagraph pencils

Because of the need to work to a minimum budget such things as food or accommodation are not included. The film-makers pay for themselves.

SHOOTING

Dates for shooting are established. The way in which a unit works will be described later. The shooting procedure must also be considered. If one is shooting synchronous sound film in the street, two people are sufficient. The important thing is that these two people, the cameraman and sound-recordist, have a strict drill to order their work.

The editor and 4-way synchronizer

The equipment is set up and the camera and tape-recorder are linked by the pulse cable. The sound-recordist plugs in and adjusts the level of the microphone. The camera is briefly started to make sure a pulse is coming through. When shooting commences the tape-recorder is always started *before* the camera.

When shooting in a studio a clapper-board is the normal method of marking the beginning of each shot. This board has the relevant information about each shot chalked on it. It also has a piece of heavy wood, hinged at one end, across its top. The wood is painted with diagonal black-and-white stripes. When the wood is brought sharply down on top of the board it makes a loud crack. This crack is recorded on both picture and sound. From this mark the editor can 'sync. up' the film before he begins to work. This is done by placing the sound of the crack over the playback head on the editing machine. The exact frame of film where the two pieces of board meet is placed in the viewfinder.

Another way of marking the beginning of the film is for the sound-recordist to stand in front of the camera and speak the relevant information into the microphone. He holds the microphone vertically in front of his chest. When he has finished speaking he brings the flat of his hand down so that it meets the microphone at right-angles. This method is suitable when the unit are working under pressure and it is not possible to use a clapper-board.

Some 16 mm. cameras have what is known as a 'silent slate' built into them. This obviates the need for a clapper-board. Every time the camera starts a small bright light blanks four or five frames of film. At the same instant a bleep is put on the tape. This makes synchronization quite simple.

BETWEEN SHOOTING AND EDITING

After shooting the film is taken to the laboratories for processing. One print or *cutting copy* is made and returned with the negative. Both the negative and cutting copy have identical numbers printed along their edges. The numbers on each reel of negative are carefully logged in a book and the negative is filed away in a cool dust-free place.

The sound is transferred from quarter-inch tape to 16 mm. magnetic film. This is also done at the laboratories.

EDITING

The first job the editor has is to synchronize sound and picture. Each sequence is numbered every few feet with a chinagraph pencil. This is done on both sound and picture and avoids trouble over the loss of synchronization.

If the editor has a rigid shooting script to follow, his job is now mainly interpretative. If the script was fairly free, he must *create* the film from the material available.

Sound and picture are edited at the same time. The cutting copy is marked by the editor to show any special effects which may be desired. These effects are known as *opticals* and include fades, dissolves, etc.

It has been mentioned before that there is usually more than one sound-track as editing progresses. The first track would be the one on which is the synchronous sound shooting. The second track may have music, effects, or a commentary on it. Each track is numbered with a chinagraph pencil. These numbers correspond with numbers on the picture.

Editing is a lengthy process involving much discussion and thought. When the cutting copy is finished it is known as the fine cut. Any titles will have been shot and cut in at this stage.

THE DUBBING SESSION

When the sound-tracks and the picture have been finalized, the next process is to mix all the sound-tracks on to one master track. This is done in the sound recording studios and is known as the dubbing session. A special chart is prepared which shows the exact footage at which a track is to fade in or out. This chart is read rather like a piece of music by the man who does the dubbing. All sound-tracks and the picture are locked together as they were in the picture synchronizer. The recording machines are usually in the projection-room. The film-makers sit in the theatre and watch the film. The sound reproduction is as good as that in a full-size theatre. It may be that this is the first time all tracks have been heard together played at the correct speed. Picture and sound may be stopped at any time and rolled backwards. Any mistakes may then be remixed without going right back to the beginning.

THE OPTICAL SOUND-TRACK

The sound is now on one reel of 16 mm. magnetic film. It has still to be combined with the picture. In order to understand what happens to the sound-track it is necessary to understand very simply how sound is reproduced when the final film is projected. Almost all commercial films have what is known as an optical sound-track. This runs down one side of the 16 mm. film and appears as a wavy line. In the projector is a photoelectric cell. A small light shines through the sound-track. The pattern on the sound-track causes the amount of light reaching the cell to vary. These variations are transformed into sounds which are greatly amplified.

The optical sound-track is printed on to the combined or 'married' print at the same time as the picture negative. In order for this to happen, the magnetic sound-track is converted into an *optical negative*. These two negatives are made into a combined print at the laboratories. The process may be repeated several times if more than one print is required.

NEGATIVE CUTTING

The picture negative has to be cut before it can be matched with the optical negative. The cutting copy is at this stage copiously marked with a chinagraph pencil and may be scratched and damaged in places. This is the time when the negative has to be brought out of store. The negative cutter has to match each shot in the film with its corresponding negative. It is a job which requires patience and skill. The edge numbers on the cutting copy are matched with the numbers on the negative. This is why it is important to keep a log of all the edge numbers and label the negative cans clearly. All negative must be handled with special gloves to ensure that no dust or grease is picked up.

This deliberately simplified explanation is designed to show the basic stages through which any professional or semi-professional film must pass. The rest of this chapter shows how a small group of film-makers tackled a particular documentary. Some of the process described will be re-examined in relation to specific practical incidents.

Ronnie Lord at work

O.K. THEN!

The acquisition of technical knowledge is the result of enthusiasm and experience. What is finally of greater importance is the ability to work with and understand the people being filmed.

This is a film about an entertainer called Ronnie Lord. He works mainly in public-houses in London. The film is shot at two main locations – a public-house and the streets of Hoxton where Ronnie Lord grew up. Two short sequences were shot in his home. The film lasts twenty-five minutes.

THE SCRIPT

The script for this film was very brief. It mentioned only locations and the fact that these different locations would be intercut in the film. Before the film was made, the film-makers had watched Ronnie Lord at work over a period of eighteen months. During this time they had seen the many different types of performance he was capable of giving. He compered each evening's performance, mimed, sang, and told jokes. He worked six nights a week and one lunch-time. The public-house in which he worked was packed every night and the audience showed disapproval of any act by ignoring it. The noise of the music was always deafening. No one went for a quiet evening.

The man himself was good-humoured and physically and mentally resilient. His manner of speech had a fluency and honesty denied to more famous performers and he was in no sense an amateur. When not on the stage he was still a straight talker with an indigenous sense of humour. The qualities he possessed did not need justification of the sort offered here, nor were they necessary as part of the script.

Spontaneous shooting in the street

SHOOTING

The film was shot in three sessions. Each of the main sessions lasted about three hours. Four people were involved in the shooting in the public-house: one person recorded sound, another operated the main camera. The third person used a non-sync. camera to shoot cutaway shots, and a fourth directed the operation. The cutaway shots are extremely important. They provide linking material between takes and also enable the editor to remove anything which may be out of focus or too shaky in a synchronous sound take.

The director ensured that the sound-recordist and cameraman were connected by the sync. pulse lead at the beginning of each shot. The sound-recordist would indicate as soon as the sync. pulse came through. Most of this was done by hand signals as it was too noisy to speak and sound-recordist and cameraman were on opposite sides of the room.

The second main shooting session was done in the streets of Hoxton. This time only two members of the unit were involved. The camera was placed on a shoulder harness which made it easily portable. The director also did the job of sound-recordist. Ronnie Lord carried a microphone with him and often spoke straight at the camera. This meant that the two unit members and Ronnie Lord were linked together by cables, with the sound-recordist in the middle. In this way it was possible for the unit to move easily and quietly through quite crowded streets, stopping wherever necessary. Working in this way the presence of the camera is often fully acknowledged. Ronnie Lord would often nod to the camera after talking to someone and say 'O.K. then – let's go down this way now. Follow us.'

In the pub

85

The third shooting session lasted just over an hour. The film was shot mute in Ronnie Lord's home.

The next process was to have the film developed and one print made. Sound and picture were synchronized and all material, both sound and mute, was viewed many times. The idea of intercutting separate locations had already been established. Editing became a process of choosing specific passages shot in the public-house and cutting them against street scenes. Quite often the sound of the public-house would be allowed to run over these scenes.

Another recording session took place and Ronnie Lord was asked to talk about himself and his job. This was done in relation to the film which he had also seen. These comments were put on a separate track. When picture and sound were finally edited and both sound-tracks completed, a dubbing chart was prepared.

At the dubbing session it was possible to readjust the sound levels at points where the sound had jumped up or down. A loop of traffic noise was also mixed into the street scenes. This helped to unify the sound. Following the dubbing session the film went through the other processes already mentioned.

The amount of film shot was twice the length of the finished film. The main point to notice is that it is possible for a very small group of people to make a film such as this. It costs less than a sixth of the normal price of a commercially made film.

Bibliography

The following books have been chosen as excellent sources of more specialized technical information:

American Cinematographer Manual (2nd ed.). The American Society of Cinematographers, Hollywood, 1968
Handbook of Amateur Cinematography, R. H. Bomback (ed.), (vols. i and ii). Fountain Press, London, 1958

The following books in the Library of Communication Techniques series. All published by the Focal Press, London and New York:

The Technique of Documentary Film Production by W. Hugh Baddeley, 1967
The Technique of Film Animation by John Hallas and Roger Manvell, 1968
The Technique of Film Editing by Karel Reisz, 1968
The Technique of Film Music by John Huntley and Roger Manvell, 1967
The Technique of Film and Television Make-up by Vincent J.-R. Kehoe, 1967
The Technique of the Sound Studio by Alec Nisbett, 1967
The Technique of Special Effects Cinematography by Raymond Fielding, 1967

The books listed below deal with the theory and aesthetics of film in a more pedantic manner or are related to specific ideas put forward in the book:

Film Making in Schools by Douglas Lowndes. Batsford, London, 1968
Hiroshima Mon Amour by Marguerite Duras. The Grove Press, London and New York, 1961
Last Year at Marienbad by Alain Robbe-Grillet. John Calder, 1965
The Contemporary Cinema by Penelope Houston. Penguin Books, London, 1963
Theory of the Film by Bela Belasz. Dennis Dobson, London, 1952
Theory of Film: The Redemption of Physical Reality by Siegfried Kracauer. Oxford University Press, 1965

Index